*The Craftsman Series*

# THE
# BELL ROCK LIGHTHOUSE

The Bell Rock Lighthouse in a storm *From a drawing by J. M. W. Turner, R.A.*

# *The*
# BELL ROCK LIGHTHOUSE

BY

ROBERT STEVENSON
*Civil Engineer*

Passages selected from
*An Account of the Bell Rock Lighthouse*
(published in 1824)

and edited by

A. F. COLLINS, B.Sc.
*Inspector of Handicraft and Science*
*Birmingham Education Authority*

CAMBRIDGE
AT THE UNIVERSITY PRESS
1931

CAMBRIDGE UNIVERSITY PRESS
Cambridge, New York, Melbourne, Madrid, Cape Town,
Singapore, São Paulo, Delhi, Mexico City

Cambridge University Press
The Edinburgh Building, Cambridge CB2 8RU, UK

Published in the United States of America by Cambridge University Press, New York

www.cambridge.org
Information on this title: www.cambridge.org/9781107610934



First published 1931
First paperback edition 2013

*A catalogue record for this publication is available from the British Library*

ISBN 978-1-107-61093-4 Paperback

# CONTENTS

## OPERATIONS OF 1809



## OPERATIONS OF 1810

# ILLUSTRATIONS

# EDITOR'S PREFACE

An examination of the literature suitable to the needs of adolescent readers and available for their use, especially in schools, brings to light the fact that it includes few books which reveal the personality of the craftsman as well as the interest of his work. Yet no reflective person can fail to realise how great a part the development of constructive activities in the sphere of material things has played in the progress of mankind.

That young people are interested in craftsmen and their work is clear from the popularity, particularly among boys, of books which describe the more spectacular achievements of the engineer and inventor. Such books are, however, for the most part written more with the aim of presenting technicalities in a popular and readable form than of showing us the craftsman himself—the man behind the work. Moreover, their literary standard is often such that they are not regarded as subjects for other than purely recreative reading.

Records of their work written by practising craftsmen, or by those who, while directing the work of others, show an intimate knowledge of a craft gained through an arduous apprenticeship, are not common. They do exist, however, and contain literature of real worth, full of human as well as of technical interest.

The object of "The Craftsman Series" is to make this literature available in a form convenient for school use, especially at the present time when so much attention is being given to the practice of the crafts as a part of general education, and to the need for a suitable literary and historical background for more specialised technical studies.

Robert Stevenson's "Account of the Bell Rock Lighthouse"

is an outstanding example of the type of literature suitable to our purpose. Stevenson often acknowledged his own debt, as an engineer, to Smeaton's "Narrative of Eddystone", and the "Account", which, as its lengthy title-page shows, was "drawn up by desire of the Commissioners of the Northern Lighthouses" and published in 1824, was clearly intended as a similar contribution to the technical records of lighthouse building.

It is a substantial folio volume containing 533 pages of text and many beautifully drawn plates, and is a monument to the thoroughness of the author. In addition to the story of the building, which is written in diary form, he includes a report upon the progress of the Northern Lighthouses, detailed technical descriptions of the various operations at the Bell Rock, and page after page of exact accounts of the material used and of its cost.

Yet, technical as is the "Account" as a whole, in the description of the progress of the building which forms the major part of the book we have a remarkably human document. It is a picture of the great engineer whose one object was to build well, and of his band of workmen who were bound to him by no mere ties of sentiment or self-interest, but by a profound respect for his ability and his unswerving devotion to duty. In reading it one feels that here indeed is a man whose character is as upright as the tower which still stands to bear testimony to his engineering ability.

The Editor's task in reducing so large a volume so as to bring it within the compass of the present pages has involved the selection of such passages as appear to be of the greatest interest to the general reader, and the joining together of these extracts to form a continuous narrative. This has occasionally necessitated the rearrangement of a sentence, a slight alteration in punctuation, or the rendering of a word into modern spelling, but apart from these insignificant changes no departure has been made from the text of the original, and throughout this book Robert Stevenson speaks for himself.

The introductory chapter, the short glossary, the occasional footnotes and linking-up passages, and the division of the text into chapters for convenience in reading, complete the Editor's contribution.

All but two of the illustrations have been reproduced from the original "Account". The portrait of Robert Stevenson, and the photograph of the lighthouse as it stands to-day, have been lent by Mr David Stevenson, a grandson of the author and his present successor in the post of Engineer to the Commissioners of Northern Lighthouses. Mr Stevenson's help has not been restricted to the lending of these illustrations, for he has shown the greatest interest in the whole project of reprinting the "Account", and has supplied valuable information concerning the present state of the lighthouse. The Editor gratefully acknowledges the help and advice he has received in these matters.

This Preface would be incomplete if the Editor were not also to acknowledge with thanks the assistance he has received from Mr C. E. Carrington, M.A., of the Cambridge University Press, in the task of seeing this edition through the printer's hands.

A. F. C.

*April 1931*

Robert Stevenson *From a painting by John Syme, R.S.A.*

# INTRODUCTION

The Abbot of Aberbrothock
Had placed that Bell on the Inchcape Rock.

THE old legend of the Bell on the Inchcape Rock is known to every reader of Southey's famous poem. Whether the story be true or false, it has given the name to the rock which it bears to this day, and it is upon this rock, the scene of so many disastrous shipwrecks, that the great lighthouse was built which is the subject of this book.

The builder, Robert Stevenson, was born in Glasgow in 1772. As a young man he acted as assistant to his stepfather, Thomas Smith of Edinburgh, in the supervision of such lighthouses as then existed on the coast of Scotland. These were few in number, and but crudely illuminated with uncertain coal fires. Thomas Smith did much to improve them by the introductions of lamps with reflectors. Young Stevenson worked hard to qualify himself as a civil engineer, and we hear of him being entrusted, at the early age of nineteen, with the building of a lighthouse on the island of Little Cumbrae in the Firth of Clyde. In 1798, after having had further experience of lighthouse building, he succeeded his stepfather as Engineer to the Commissioners of Northern Lighthouses. He remained in this service until his retirement in 1843, devoting much energy to the improvement of lighthouses, and it was early in this period that he carried out the work of which he tells the story in these pages. His practice as a civil engineer also included harbour construction, bridge building and river improvements, but it is as a lighthouse builder that his name is best known.

Building is one of the oldest of human handicrafts, and all over the world castles, towers, cathedrals and other fine structures stand to testify to the skill which men had attained in this art long before the days of the Bell Rock Lighthouse. But the work which Stevenson began in 1807 was unlike any building which had then been attempted. Until that time no one had ever tried to build a strong tower upon a rock which was eleven miles from the nearest land, in the midst of stormy seas which barely uncovered it at low tide.

It is true that in 1759, nearly fifty years before, Smeaton had completed the first stone tower on the Eddystone Rock, fourteen miles off Plymouth, but the Eddystone was only just covered by the highest tides, whereas the Bell Rock was twice daily submerged to a depth of from twelve to sixteen feet.

We must remember that Stevenson and his men accomplished their work without the aids which modern builders would bring to such an undertaking. In 1807 the steamboat was a curiosity, not yet brought to practical use, and only small sailing vessels were available. The use of steam power for working the tackle for raising the stones was unknown, and even the cranes themselves had to be specially devised for the work. Stevenson foresaw this difficulty of the lack of suitable cranes, for in one of his notebooks he wrote "... morning, noon and night these difficulties have haunted me". To solve his problems he invented two special cranes; the jib or movable beam crane, which is now so common an object in all building operations, and the balance-crane for use at the top of the lighthouse building.

So stormy were the seas around the exposed position of the Bell Rock that work could only be carried on during the summer months, and, for the first two years, until the building had reached a sufficient height above the waves, only for a few hours each day while the tide was low. Even so, in the early stages of the building, rough weather often put a stop to the work for days together, during which time Stevenson and his men had to stay on board of their tiny ship in conditions of the utmost discomfort, waiting for the weather to improve. When it did improve, their only relief from the ceaseless tossing of the waves was to snatch a few hours' work on the sea-washed rock before the rising tide drove them back to their close quarters for another long wait.

The story is one long record of hardships and dangers cheerfully borne by men whose one determination was to do their work well.

Throughout the book we see Robert Stevenson, the master craftsman, carefully planning every step of the work in advance; watching over every operation with the closest attention; the first to land and the last to leave the rock, sharing his men's dangers and discomforts and ever mindful of their safety and well-being.

No wonder that we are assured by those who knew him that Robert Stevenson was esteemed above all others by his workmen, many of whom continued in his service for many years after the Bell Rock Lighthouse was completed.

In reading the story we cannot fail to be impressed by Stevenson's modesty and singleness of purpose. To him the success of the work was all that mattered, and, were he alive to-day, he would be the first to say that his men were, equally with himself, the true heroes of the story. Skilled masons, smiths and carpenters, taken from the workshops and work-yards ashore to spend their hours of work in unremitting toil upon an exposed rock, and their hours of leisure cooped up in the hold of a tiny sailing vessel, these men proved themselves worthy co-workers with the great engineer who was their leader. Stevenson gives us many glimpses of the characters of these men. We read of George Forsyth, to whom the motion of the ship "was death itself", and who preferred to spend his nights alone "with a small black dog" in the unfinished beacon-house perched upon stilts above the raging seas—surely one of the strangest habitations ever built by civilised man.

Another is Peter Fortune, the versatile and good-natured "cook, steward, surgeon and barber"; another, James Glen, who with tales of his own earlier hardships reconciled his mates to the terrible discomforts of their situation when they were marooned upon the beacon. Also there are the four men who, for conscience' sake, declined to work on Sundays, but who were among the first to volunteer for work at the rock when their fellows, alarmed by their narrow escape from drowning on the previous day, hesitated to leave the ship.

And so throughout the story we see that these men were very real people to their leader Stevenson; they were not merely "hands" to do his will.

How well this band of sixty men did their work is best shown in the words of Mr David Stevenson, the grandson of Robert Stevenson and the present Engineer to the Northern Lighthouse Board. Writing in 1930, he says: "The Bell Rock Lighthouse is now the oldest seawashed tower in existence, and the masonry stands exactly as Stevenson designed and completed it. It has required no repair whatever during the 119 years which have elapsed since it was built. The only changes that have been made are in the arrangements for fog signalling and for the light itself, which were modernised in 1902, when a much larger lantern was built". A comparison of the pictures on pages 127 and 132 will show these changes in the lantern.

Robert Stevenson was the first of a great family of lighthouse engineers. After him three of his sons in succession took over the duties of Engineer to the Northern Lighthouse Board, and for the last forty years his grandson has held the position. Other members of the family are also connected with this work, and since Robert's time the name of Stevenson has always been an honoured one in lighthouse engineering. "The courage, wisdom, and other fine qualities", writes Mr David Stevenson, "with which Robert Stevenson was endowed were an inspiration to his sons who succeeded him and to his grandson. I trust and believe that they will inspire the young people who read this volume."

Robert Louis Stevenson, the famous writer, best known to boys as the author of "Treasure Island", was a grandson of Robert Stevenson, and as a young man intended to become a lighthouse engineer, until his health compelled him to give up the idea. "R. L. S." has given us a charming description of his grandfather in his book "Records of a Family of Engineers", in which he speaks highly of the "Account of the Bell Rock Lighthouse" and quotes freely from it.

In the pages which follow you will be able to read for yourself Robert Stevenson's own record of a great task nobly accomplished.

# GLOSSARY

ARCANUM OF VULCAN. The mystery or secret of the smith's trade. Vulcan was the ancient Romans' god of fire and metalwork.

BALLAST. Heavy material placed in a ship's hold to weight the vessel so that it will sail properly, especially when no other cargo is being carried.

BOWER-ANCHOR. One of the anchors carried at the bow or forward part of a ship.

BUSH. A metal lining or bearing for an axle, such as that of a windlass. When 'the bolt of the bush gave way' (p. 101) the axle of the machine became loose and let the stone fall.

COXWAIN. The man who steers a boat.

COURSE. One of the horizontal layers in which bricks or stones are laid when a building is being erected.

CUTTER. A small single-masted sailing vessel, with a rigging somewhat different from that of a sloop. (See 'Sloop'.)

DAVITS. A pair of curved arms forming a kind of crane, used for lowering a small boat into the water from a ship's side.

DEAD-LIGHT. A shutter to protect a cabin window, skylight, or porthole from the force of the sea.

DOVETAILING. A method of joining wood or stone in which one piece, shaped like a dove's tail or reversed wedge, is fitted tightly into a corresponding hole in another piece, thus locking the two parts together. (See illustration on p. 54.) The method is very common in woodwork; dovetails may be seen at the sides of any drawer. In masonry it is used only for special buildings such as lighthouses which have to withstand great shocks.

DULSE. A kind of edible seaweed.

EMBARGO. An order forbidding ships to enter or leave port.

FREESTONE MASONS. The men who worked the sandstone, as distinct from those who worked the harder granite (the granite masons).

FUCI. Seaweed with flat leathery leaves or fronds.

GALLEY. A ship's kitchen.

GROUND-TACKLE. The anchors and cables by which a ship is moored or anchored.

GROUTING. Pouring thin fluid mortar into the joints between the stones. It percolates into crevices which could not be reached with the trowel, and afterwards sets hard, forming a solid joint.

GUNWALE. The upper edge of a boat's side.

GUY-TACKLES. The ropes or 'tackle' used as stays to hold the upright beams of the crane in place.

HAWSER. A heavy rope or cable used to moor a ship.

HELM. The tiller or wheel by which the rudder of a ship is controlled and the vessel is steered.

JOGGLES. The small stones let in between each course or layer of masonry, to prevent one course sliding over the other. They can be seen in the section on p. 129.

JOISTINGS. The cross beams upon which the boards of a floor are nailed.

JUMPER. A steel rod or chisel used for boring holes in rock or stone. It is held in position and repeatedly struck with a hammer. Between each hammer-blow it is 'jumped' or turned slightly, so that the cutting edge gradually eats its way into the rock.

KEDGE-ANCHOR. To 'kedge' a ship is to move it by winding in a cable fastened to a small anchor (the kedge-anchor) sunk at a distance from the original position of the vessel.

LEEWARD. Away from the wind; in the direction towards which the wind is blowing (cf. 'Windward'). The lee side is the quiet or sheltered side of a ship or rock.

LEWIS-BAT. A wedge-shaped iron device for attaching a chain or rope to a block of stone for the purpose of lifting it.

LIMBERS. Holes cut in the floor-timbers of a ship to allow water to drain into the well of the ship's pumps.

LINKS. An old name for torches.

MORTISED. The upper ends of the main beams of the beacon were let into holes ('mortises') cut in the central block of wood. The 'mortise and tenon' joint is very common in woodwork, especially in framing of all kinds.

POZZOLANO. A kind of cement which will set solid under water.

PURCHASE-TACKLE. An arrangement of ropes and pulleys used for hoisting heavy weights.

REGISTER TONS. The 'tonnage' or capacity of every ship is entered in the official Register of Shipping. It was upon this 'Registered Tonnage' that the amount of Lighthouse Duty to be collected from each ship was calculated.

SAW-DRAUGHT. A saw-cut.

SCUTTLES. Holes, with lids over them, in a ship's deck or side. When waves break over the deck the water is allowed to escape into the sea or into the well of the ship's pumps by opening the scuttles.

SLOOP. A small single-masted sailing vessel rigged with a large four-sided 'mainsail' and a smaller triangular 'jib' or 'foresail'.

STANCHION. An upright post or pillar.

THWARTS. The cross benches or seats of a boat, upon which the rowers sit.

WAIST (of a ship). The central part of the vessel, midway between the 'forecastle' (forward) and the 'quarterdeck' (aft).

WINCH-MACHINE. A machine used for hauling ropes or chains by winding them upon a drum. It is similar to a windlass. At the Bell Rock the winches were turned by hand, using a crank; nowadays many winches are steam-driven.

WINDWARD. Towards the wind; in the direction from which the wind is coming (cf. 'Leeward'). The windward side is the windy or exposed side of a ship or rock.

# THE BELL ROCK

## *CHAPTER I*

## Situation and character of the Bell Rock. Proposal for a lighthouse to be erected. The floating-light prepared and moored.

(The Bell Rock was formerly known as the Inchcape Rock.)

The Bell Rock may be described as a most dangerous sunken reef, situate on the northern side of the entrance of the great estuary or arm of the sea called the Frith of Forth; and as such directly affecting the safety of all vessels entering the Frith of Tay. The surface of the rock is rugged and full of cavities, so that walking upon it becomes rather difficult.

At the time of high-water of spring-tides[1] the south-western reef is about 16 feet, or nearly the whole rise of the tide, under the surface of the water; while the part of the rock on which the lighthouse is built is about 12 feet below high-water mark of spring-tides; at low-water of neap-tides, hardly any part of the rock is visible: but at low-water of spring-tides, the general level of the north-eastern end where the lighthouse is built is about four feet perpendicular above the level of the sea.

Whatever may have been the early state of the Inch Cape or Bell Rock as an island, its present character is strictly that of a sunken rock; and, as such, its relative situation on the eastern shores of Great Britain has long rendered it one of the chief impediments to the free navigation of that coast.

[1] 'Spring' and 'neap' tides occur in alternate weeks. In spring tides the range between high and low water is at its maximum; in neap tides at its minimum.

The disastrous shipwrecks which occasionally happened at the entrance of the Friths of Forth and Tay deeply impressed every one conversant in nautical affairs with the most convincing proofs of the necessity for some distinguishing mark being erected upon the Bell Rock. As yet, the writer had not landed upon the rock; though he had begun to prepare a model of a pillar-formed lighthouse, to be supported upon six columns of cast-iron, under the impression that this description of building was alone suitable to its situation. In the summer of the year 1800, this model was presented to the Lighthouse Board, when an official application was made to the Commissioners of his Majesty's Customs for the use of the Osnaburgh cutter, then lying in the harbour of Elie, on the coast of Fife, to carry the writer to the Bell Rock, that, by landing there, he might be enabled to judge of the applicability of his pillar-formed design to the situation of the rock. Upon reaching Elie, the Osnaburgh was found to be under repair, and could not possibly go to sea for several days, by which time the spring-tides would be over. The journey was continued along the coast to West Haven, on the northern side of the Frith of Tay, where a large boat was procured, and manned with fishermen who were in the habit of visiting the rock to search for articles of shipwreck.

On this first visit to the Bell Rock, the writer was accompanied by his friend Mr James Haldane, architect. The crew being unwilling to risk their boat into any of the creeks in the rock, very properly observing that the lives of all depended upon her safety, and as we could only remain upon the rock for two or three hours at most, we landed upon a shelving part on the south side of the rock. Having been extremely fortunate both as to the state of the weather and tides, an opportunity was afforded of making a sketch of the rock at low-water: meantime, the boatmen were busily employed in searching all the

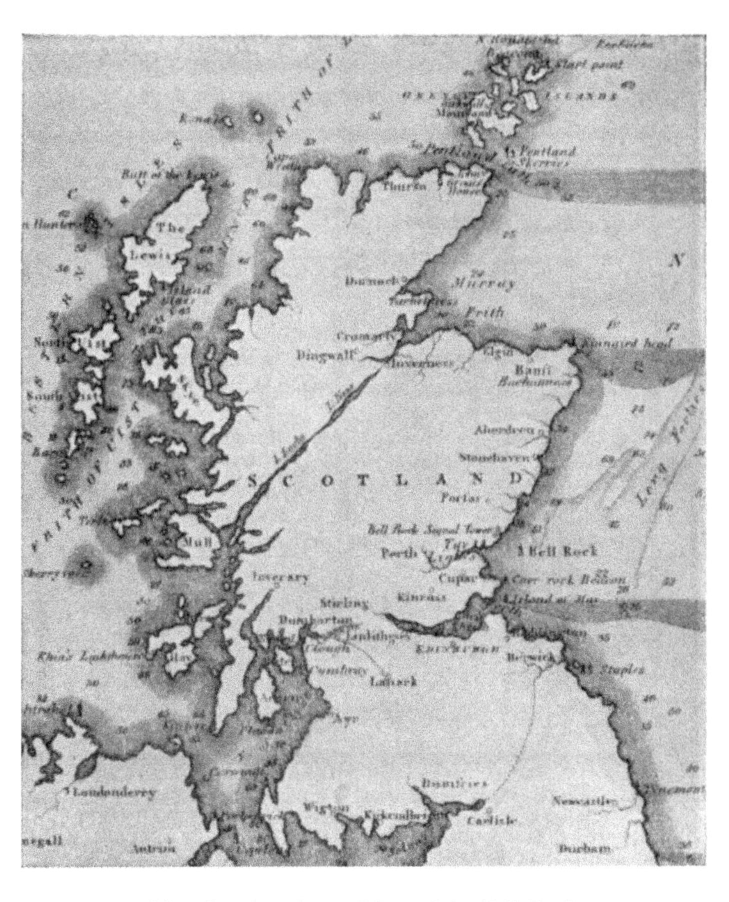


Map showing the position of the Bell Rock
on the coast of Scotland

holes and crevices in quest of articles of shipwreck, and by the time that the tide overflowed the rock, they had collected upwards of two cwt. of old metal, consisting of such things as are used on shipboard. A few of these were kept by the writer, such

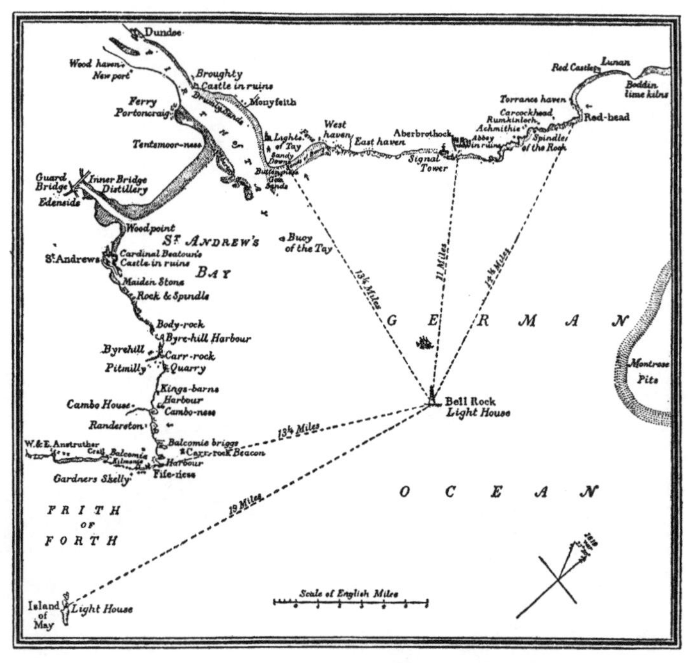


Chart showing the distance of the Bell Rock
from the coast of the Firths of Forth and Tay

as a hinge and lock of a door, a ship's marking-iron, a piece of a ship's caboose (or *kambuis*, cover of the cooking-place), a soldier's bayonet, a cannon ball, several pieces of money, a shoe-buckle, &c.; while the heavier and more bulky articles, as a piece of a kedge-anchor, cabin-stove, crowbars, &c. were left with the crew.

The immediate result of this visit on the mind of the writer and of Mr Haldane was a firm conviction of the practicability of erecting a building of stone upon the Bell Rock; and from that moment the idea of a pillar-formed lighthouse was rejected, as unsuitable to the situation. Under these impressions, the writer, after his first visit to the Bell Rock, in the year 1800, made a variety of drawings, and constructed new models for a building of stone, shewing various methods of connecting the stones by dove-tailing them laterally, like those of the Eddystone Lighthouse, and also course to course into one another perpendicularly. These plans and models were duly submitted to the Lighthouse Board, accompanied with estimates of the expence, amounting to the maximum sum of £42,685, 8*s*.

(One notices the care with which Stevenson must have worked out his costs. To estimate to the nearest shilling for so great an undertaking was indeed a remarkable performance.

The Commissioners of Northern Lighthouses promoted a Bill in Parliament to empower them to levy a duty upon shipping in the neighbourhood of the Bell Rock, for the purpose of raising funds to build a lighthouse upon the rock.)

The Act of Parliament, by which the Commissioners of the Northern Lighthouses were empowered to undertake the works at the Bell Rock, having only received the Royal Assent late in the month of July 1806, there was not sufficient time for making the necessary preparations for their commencement that season. But the writer, on his return from London, received instructions from the Board to have such preliminary steps in view as would enable him to begin the operations early in the summer of 1807.

The bill for the Bell Rock Lighthouse was drawn up under a strong impression of the uncertainty which must attend the whole of the works at the rock, and doubts were accordingly entertained as to the estimated expense being adequate to the accomplishment of the undertaking. A clause had, therefore, been introduced, authorising the collection of lighthouse duties of one penny halfpenny *per* register ton from British vessels and threepence *per* ton from foreigners, 'immediately upon mooring or anchoring a ship or vessel, and exhibiting a floating or other light, at or near the Bell Rock', and 'half the amount of the said duties respectively', on the erection of 'a proper beacon or distinguishing mark or object on the said Bell Rock'. The measures first in order were, consequently, to fit out and moor a floating-light and to erect a beacon on the Bell Rock, that shipping might derive immediate advantage from them while the lighthouse was in progress; and also that the funds of the Board might, as early as possible, have the benefit of the additional duties.

In the year 1806, a great number of vessels were taken by our cruisers upon the coasts of Holland, Denmark and Norway, many of which were carried into Leith to be sold. One of these, a Prussian, which happened to be captured while fishing on the Dogger Bank, was purchased for the Bell Rock service. She was called the Tonge Gerrit, but was afterwards named the Pharos, in allusion to the celebrated Pharos of Alexandria.[1]

(This vessel was specially fitted up to serve as a lightship, and after some difficulty, was anchored about one-and-a-half miles northwest of the Bell Rock on 14th July, 1807. After lying at anchor for some weeks to test the moorings, a light was exhibited from the Pharos on 15th September, 1807.)

[1] *The Pharos of Alexandria was a famous beacon-tower built in Egypt about 250* B.C., *and then regarded as one of the wonders of the world.*

# OPERATIONS OF 1807

## CHAPTER II

## The Smeaton built and launched. A preliminary trip to the rock. Selection of artificers. The working party sails to the rock.

We shall first proceed to a detail of the operations *afloat*, as they may be termed, or of the works upon the rock itself, during the season of 1807,—particularly of the erection of the principal beams of the beacon-house, or temporary residence for the artificers on the rock, and of the progress made in the preparation of the foundation or site of the main building. We therefore observe, that a vessel had been built at Leith, in the course of the spring, expressly for the Bell Rock service, to be employed as a tender for the floating-light, and as a stone-lighter for the use of the work. This vessel was launched in the month of June; she measured 40 tons register, was rigged as a sloop, and fitted in all respects in the strongest manner, to adapt her as much as possible for the perilous service in which she was to be employed. She was called The Smeaton,—a name which the writer had great pleasure in suggesting, as a mark of respect for the memory of the celebrated engineer of the Eddystone Lighthouse, whose narrative was to become a kind of text-book for the Bell Rock operations. The Smeaton was ready for sea in the beginning of August, and reached Arbroath upon the 5th day of that month.

The floating-light rode in safety at her moorings, and had hitherto been supplied with necessaries by the yacht belonging to the general service of the Lighthouse Board. In this vessel, occasional trips had also been made to the rock. In these

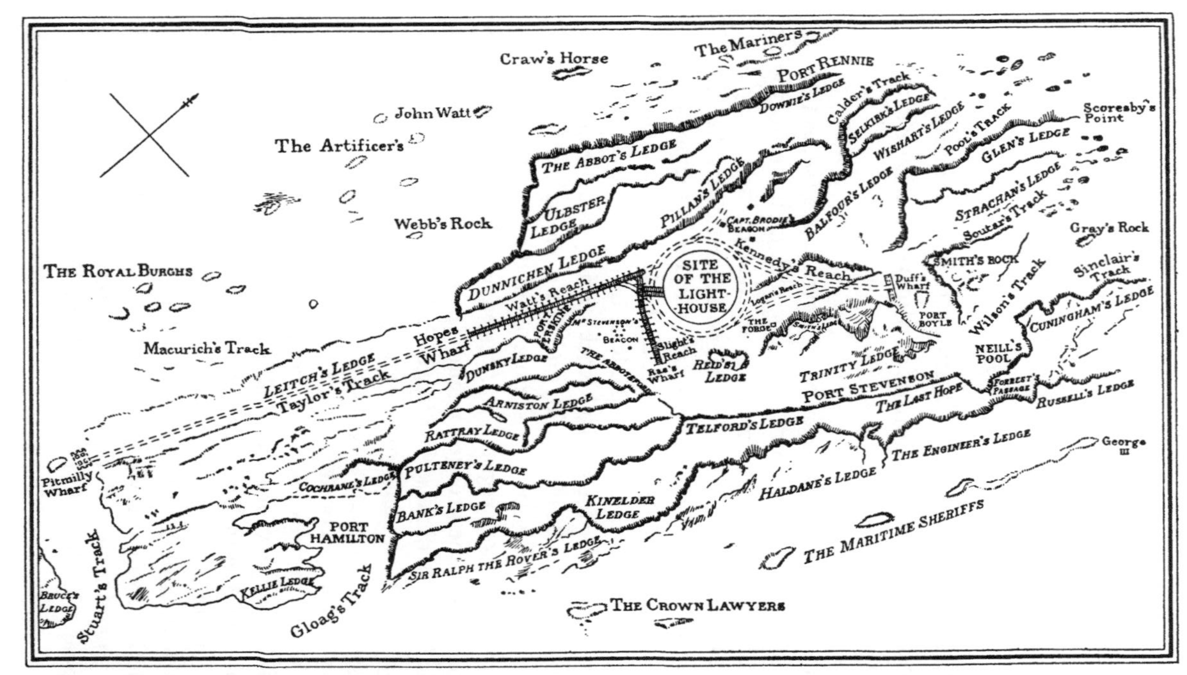


Plan of the north-east part of the Bell Rock, showing the site of the lighthouse. (Many parts of the rock were named after members of the working-party)

preliminary trips the writer had fixed in his own mind upon the parts of the rock most favourable for the position of the lighthouse, and on the south-west of it he chose the site of the beacon-house, that it might be sheltered in some measure from the breach of the north-east sea.

The Smeaton having got on board necessaries for the floating-light, and three sets of chain-moorings with mushroom-anchors and large floating buoys, the writer sailed on another preliminary visit to the Bell Rock on the 7th day of August, carrying with him Mr Peter Logan, foreman builder, and five artificers, selected, on this occasion, from their having been somewhat accustomed to the sea; the writer being aware of the distressing trial which the floating-light would necessarily inflict upon landsmen, from her rolling motion. Here he remained till the 10th, and as the weather was favourable, a landing was effected daily, when the workmen were employed in cutting the large sea-weed from the sites of the lighthouse and beacon, which were respectively traced with pick-axes upon the rock. In the meantime, the crew of the Smeaton was employed in laying down the several sets of moorings within half a mile of the rock, for the convenience of vessels riding at the buoys by a hawser, instead of letting go an anchor.

The artificers, having fortunately experienced moderate weather, returned to the work-yard at Arbroath with a good report of their treatment afloat; when their comrades ashore began to feel some anxiety to see a place of which they had heard so much, and to change the constant operation with the iron and mallet in the process of hewing, for an occasional tide's work on the rock, which they figured to themselves as a state of comparative ease and comfort. In answer to some advances which had been made on this subject by the artificers, the foreman was instructed to select fourteen of the stone-cutters who had been accustomed to the use of the pick-axe, and to boring or drilling holes with a jumper after the manner of quarriers, to go off to the rock in the course of a few days. In any agreement to be entered into, it was held as an express condition, 'That every man who embarked for the work at the Bell Rock should remain for the space of four weeks, without returning ashore'. Those chiefly wanted at this time were masons from Aberdeen, who were accustomed to the use of the boring-iron and pick in working granite. Being engaged only from week to week in the work-yard, they were desirous of knowing the reason for remaining a month at the rock; when they were informed that it was not unlikely some of them might suffer from sea sickness, and wearying of confinement on board of ship might wish to return ashore, which would be attended with much inconvenience to the work, by too frequent a change of hands. They were further told that by continuing for one month afloat, they would in the course of that time become so sea-hardy as probably to feel no desire to return till the end of the working-season, which at this advanced period could not last for many weeks. This condition was considered of importance in the commencement of the work, and it was the more readily agreed to, as the writer assured them that he should himself remain with them during that period.

16TH AUGUST. Everything being arranged for sailing to the rock on Saturday the 15th, the vessel might have proceeded on the Sunday; but understanding that this would not be so agreeable to the artificers it was deferred until Monday. Here we cannot help observing, that the men allotted for the operations at the rock seemed to enter upon the undertaking with a degree of consideration which fully marked their opinion as to the hazardous nature of the undertaking on which they were about to enter. They went in a body to church on Sunday, and whether it was in the ordinary course, or designed for the occasion, the writer is not certain, but the service was in many respects suitable to their circumstances. Indeed, the Reverend Mr Gleg, the minister of the parish, was in the constant habit of enquiring after the success and safety of the works.

The tide happening to fall late in the evening of Monday the 17th, the party, counting twenty-four in number, embarked on board of the Smeaton about 10 o'clock p.m., and sailed from Arbroath with a gentle breeze at west. Our ship's colours having been flying all day in compliment to the commencement of the work, the other vessels in the harbour also saluted, which made a very gay appearance. A number of the friends and acquaintances of those on board having been thus collected, the piers, though at a late hour, were perfectly crowded, and just as the Smeaton cleared the harbour, all on board united in giving three hearty cheers, which were returned by those on shore in such good earnest, that in the still of the evening the sound must have been heard in all parts of the town, re-echoing from the walls and lofty turrets of the venerable Abbey of Aberbrothwick. The writer felt much satisfaction at the manner of this parting scene; though he must own that the present rejoicing was, on his part, mingled with occasional reflections upon the responsibility of his situation, which extended to the safety of all who should be engaged in this perilous work. With such sensations he retired to his cabin; but as the artificers were rather inclined to move about the deck then to remain in their confined berths below, his repose was transient, and the vessel being small, every motion was necessarily heard. Some who were musically inclined occasionally sung; but he listened with peculiar pleasure to the sailor at the helm, who hummed over Dibdin's characteristic air,

> They say there's a Providence sits up aloft,
> To keep watch for the life of Poor Jack.

## *CHAPTER III*

## Preparations for the beacon. The smith at work on the rock.

18TH AUGUST. The weather had been very gentle all night, and, about four in the morning of the 18th, the Smeaton anchored on the spot where it was intended to lay down an additional set of chain-moorings which she had on board. Agreeably to an arranged plan of operations, all hands were called at 5 o'clock, a.m., just as the highest part of the Bell Rock began to shew its sable head among the light breakers, which occasionally whitened with the foaming sea. The two boats belonging to the floating-light attended the Smeaton, to carry the artificers to the rock, as her boat could only accommodate about six or eight sitters. Every one was more eager than his neighbour to leap into the boats, and it required a good deal of management on the part of the coxswains to get men unaccustomed to a boat to take their places for rowing and at the same time trimming her properly. The landing-master and foreman went into one boat, while the writer took charge of another and steered it to and from the rock.

As the weather was extremely fine, with light airs of wind from the east, we landed without difficulty upon the central part of the rock at half-past 5, but the water had not yet sufficiently left it for commencing the work. This interval, however, did not pass unoccupied; the first and last of all the principal operations at the Bell Rock were accompanied by three hearty cheers from all hands, and, on occasions like the present, the steward of the ship attended, when each man was regaled with a glass of rum. As the water left the rock about 6, some began to bore the holes for the great bats or holdfasts for fixing the beams of the beacon-house, while the smith was fully attended in laying out the site of his forge upon a somewhat sheltered spot of the rock, which also recommended itself from the vicinity of a pool of water for tempering his irons. These preliminary steps occupied about an hour, and as nothing further could be done during this tide towards fixing the forge, the workmen gratified their curiosity by roaming about the rock, which they investigated with great eagerness till the tide overflowed it. Those who had been sick picked dulse (*Fucus palmatus*), which they ate with much seeming appetite; others were more intent upon collecting limpets for bait, to enjoy the amusement of fishing when they returned on board of the vessel. Indeed none came away empty handed, as everything found upon the Bell Rock was considered valuable, being connected with some interesting association. Several coins and numerous bits of shipwrecked iron were picked up, of almost every description; and, in particular, a marking-iron lettered JAMES,—a circumstance of which it was thought proper to give notice to the public, as it might lead to the knowledge of some unfortunate shipwreck, perhaps unheard of till this simple occurrence led to the discovery. When the rock began to be overflowed, the landing-master arranged the crews of the respective boats, appointing twelve persons to each. According to a rule, which the writer had laid down to himself, he was always the last person who left the rock.

In a short time, the Bell Rock was laid completely under water, and the weather being extremely fine, the sea was so smooth that its place could not be pointed out from the appearance of the surface,—a circumstance which sufficiently demonstrates the dangerous nature of this rock, even during the day and in the smoothest and calmest state of the sea. During the interval between the morning and the evening tides the artificers were variously employed in fishing and reading, others were busy in drying and adjusting their wet clothes, and one or two amused their companions with the violin and German-flute.

About 7 in the evening the signal bell for landing on the rock was again rung, when every man was at his quarters. In this service it was thought more appropriate to use the bell than to *pipe* to quarters, as the use of this instrument is less known to the mechanic than the sound of the bell. The landing, as in the morning, was at the eastern harbour. During this tide the sea-weed was pretty well cleared from the site of the operations, and also from the tracks leading to the different landing-places; for walking upon the rugged surface of the Bell Rock, when covered with sea-weed, was found to be extremely difficult and even dangerous. Every hand that could possibly be occupied, was now employed in assisting the smith to fit up the apparatus for his forge. The frame-work of iron forming the hearth was now got into its place; and the four legs which supported it were let into holes bored from six to twelve inches into the rock, according to the inequalities of the site; and then firmly wedged, first with wood, and then with iron, a method followed in all the operations of batting at the Bell Rock, and found greatly preferable to running in melted lead. The block of timber for supporting the anvil was fixed in the same manner, on which the anvil was simply laid, without any other fixture than the small stud, fitted as usual into its seat, depending upon the gravity of the mass for preserving its place against the effects of the sea. In this state things were left on the rock at 9 p.m., when the boats returned to the tender, after other two hours' work, in the same order as formerly, perhaps as much gratified with the success that attended the work of this day as with any other in the whole course of the operations.

19TH AUGUST. The boats left the ship at a quarter before 7 this morning, and landed upon the rock at 7. The boat which the writer steered happened to be the last which approached the rock at this tide; and, in standing up in the stern, while at some distance, to see how the leading boat entered the creek, he was astonished to observe something in the form of a human figure in a reclining posture upon one of the ledges of the rock. He immediately steered the boat through a narrow entrance to the eastern harbour, with a thousand unpleasant sensations in his mind. He thought a vessel or boat must have been wrecked upon the rock during the night; and it seemed probable that the rock might be strewed with dead bodies, a spectacle which could not fail to deter the artificers from returning so freely to their work. Even one individual found in this situation would naturally cast a damp upon their minds, and, at all events, make them much more timid in their future operations. In the midst of these reveries the boat took the ground at an improper landing place; but, without waiting to push her off, he leapt upon the rock, and making his way hastily to the spot which had privately given him alarm, he had the satisfaction to ascertain that he had only been deceived by the peculiar situation and aspect of the smith's anvil and block, which very completely represented the appearance of a lifeless body upon the rock. The writer carefully suppressed his feelings, the simple mention of which might have had a bad effect upon the artificers, and his haste passed for an anxiety to examine the apparatus of the smith's forge left in an unfinished state at the evening tide.

The weather being clear in the evening, the boats landed again at half-past 6 o'clock, when the artificers were employed for two hours, as in the morning, and returned again to the ship about a quarter past 8. The remainder of the day-light was eagerly spent in catching fish, which were got at this time in great abundance, both alongside of the vessel and in the boats at a distance; and in the course of an hour about five dozen of codlings were caught, which not only afforded an agreeable relaxation, but afforded a plentiful dish of fish for the different messes on board.

20TH AUGUST. In the evening the artificers landed at half-past 7, and continued till half-past 8, having completed the fixing of the smith's forge, his vice, and a wooden board or bench, which were also batted to a ledge of the rock, to the great joy of all, under a salute of three hearty cheers. From an oversight on the part of the smith, who had neglected to bring his tinder-box and matches from the vessel, the work was prevented from being continued for at least an hour longer.

It may here be proper to notice that although a considerable quantity of jumpers or boring-irons, picks, and other quarry-tools had been brought in good order for the use of the work; yet, from the extent of work in preparing the foundations, together with the hard and compact nature of the sandstone of which the Bell Rock is composed, the tools soon became blunt, and the work must have often been completely at a stand, had it not been for the convenience of having a smith and his forge so near at hand. The writer doubts not that his readers may be at a loss to account for the operation of the bellows and other apparatus upon a sunken rock, and it may therefore be necessary to give some explanation of this *arcanum* of Vulcan, on which the work had so great a dependence. The smith's shop was of course in *open space*: the large bellows were carried to and from the rock every tide, for the serviceable condition of which, together with the tinder-box, fuel and embers of the former fire, the smith was held responsible. It often happened, to our annoyance and disappointment, in the early state of the work, when the smith was in the middle of a *favourite heat* in making some useful article or in sharpening the tools, after the flood-tide had obliged the pickmen to strike work, a sea would come rolling over the rocks, dash out the fire, and endanger his indispensable implement the bellows. If the sea was smooth, while the smith often stood at work knee-deep in water, the tide rose by imperceptible degrees, first cooling the exterior of the fire-place, or hearth, and then quietly blackening and extinguishing the fire from below. The writer has frequently been amused at the perplexing anxiety of the blacksmith when coaxing his fire, and endeavouring to avert the effects of the rising tide. In this state of things, the erection of the beacon was looked forward to as a happy period when the smith should be removed above the reach of the highest tides.

## *CHAPTER IV*

## The artificers transfer to the floating-light. The first week-end afloat.

21ST AUGUST. Everything connected with the forge being now completed, the artificers found no want of sharp tools, and the work went forward with great alacrity and spirit. It was also alleged that the rock had a more habitable appearance from the volumes of smoke which ascended from the smith's shop; and the busy noise of his anvil; the operations of the masons; the movements of the boats, and shipping at a distance, all contributed to give life and activity to the scene. This noise and traffic had, however, the effect of almost completely banishing the herd of seals which had hitherto frequented the rock as a resting place during the period of low water.

We had now been six days out from Arbroath, and in that time had the good fortune to have seven successive tides' work upon the rock, during which the smith's forge had been fixed, and twelve holes of 2 inches in diameter and 18 inches in depth had been bored or drilled into the rock, in the process of excavating the bat or stanchion-holes for fixing the principal beams of the beacon-house. Hitherto the artificers had remained on board of the Smeaton, which was made fast to one of the mooring buoys at the distance only of about a quarter of a mile from the rock, and was of course a very great convenience to the work.

But the Smeaton being only about forty register tons, her accommodation was extremely limited. It may, therefore, be easily imagined that an addition of twenty-four persons to her own crew must have rendered the situation of those on board rather uncomfortable. The only place for the men's hammocks on board being in the hold, they were unavoidably much crowded; and if the weather had required the hatches to be fastened down so great a number of men could not possibly have been accommodated. To add to this evil, the caboose or cooking place being upon deck, it would not have been possible to have cooked for so large a company in the event of bad weather.

The stock of water was now getting short, and some necessaries being also wanted for the floating-light, the Smeaton was dispatched for Arbroath; and the writer with the artificers, at the same time, shifted their quarters from her to the floating-light.

22ND AUGUST. Although the rock barely made its appearance at this period of the tides till 8 o'clock, yet, having now a full mile to row from the floating-light to the rock, instead of about a quarter of a mile from the moorings of the Smeaton, it was necessary to be earlier astir and to form different arrangements; breakfast was accordingly served up at 7 o'clock this morning. From the excessive motion of the floating-light, the writer had looked forward rather with anxiety to the removal of the workmen to this ship. Some among them, who had been congratulating themselves upon having become sea-hardy while on board of the Smeaton, had a complete relapse on returning to the floating-light. This was also the case with the writer. The act of getting into or out of a boat, when alongside of the floating-light, was at all times attended with more or less difficulty; her rolling motion was so great, that the gunwale, though about five feet above the surface of the water, dipped nearly into it, upon the one side, while her keel could not be far from the surface on the other. When the tide bell rung the boats were hoisted out, and two active seamen were employed to keep them from receiving damage alongside. The floating-light, being very buoyant, was so quick in her motions that when those who were about to step from her gunwale into a boat placed themselves upon a cleat or step on the ship's side, with the man or rail ropes in their hands, they had often to wait for some time till a favourable opportunity occurred for stepping into the boat. While in this situation, with the vessel rolling from side to side, watching the proper time for letting go the man-ropes, it required the greatest dexterity and presence of mind to leap into the boat. One who was rather awkward would often wait a considerable period in this position: at one time his side of the ship would be so depressed that he would touch the boat to which he belonged while the next sea would elevate him so much that he would see his comrades in the boat on the opposite side of the ship, his friends in the one boat calling him to 'Jump', while those in the boat on the other side, as he came again and again into their view, would jocosely say, 'Are you there yet? You seem to enjoy a swing'. In this situation it was common to see a person upon each side of the ship, for a length of time, waiting to quit his hold. A stranger to this sort of motion was both alarmed for the safety, and delighted with the agility of persons leaping into the boat under those perilous circumstances. No sooner had one quitted his station on the gunwale, than another occupied his place, until the whole were safely shipped.

On leaving the rock today, a trial of seamanship was proposed amongst the rowers, for by this time the artificers had become tolerably expert in this exercise. The men, upon the whole, had but little work to perform in the course of a day; for though they exerted themselves extremely hard while on the rock, yet, in the early state of the operations, this could not be continued for more than three or four hours at a time, and as their rations were large, they got into excellent spirits when free of sea-sickness.

This being the first Saturday that the artificers were afloat, all hands were served with a glass of rum and water at night, to drink the sailors' favourite toast of 'Wives and Sweethearts'. It was customary, upon these occasions, for the seamen and artificers to collect in the galley, when the musical instruments were put in requisition; for, according to invariable practice, every man must play a tune, sing a song, or tell a story. In this manner Saturday night, in particular, passed away in a very happy manner, when much boisterous mirth and loud peals of laughter occasionally broke forth. It is true that this could not proceed from a single glass, but every man sat down with a determination to be pleased.

23RD AUGUST. To some it may require an apology, or at least call for an explanation, why the writer took upon himself to step aside from the established rules of society by carrying on the works of this undertaking during Sundays. Surely, if under any circumstances it is allowable to go about the ordinary labours of mankind on Sundays, that of the erection of a lighthouse upon the Bell Rock seems to be one of the most pressing calls which could in any case occur, and carries along with it the imperious language of necessity. In this perilous work, to give up every seventh day would just have been to protract the time a seventh part. The writer, therefore, felt little scruple in continuing the Bell Rock works in all favourable states of the weather.

At 8 o'clock all hands were assembled on the quarter-deck for prayers, a solemnity which was gone through in as orderly a manner as circumstances would admit.

Some demur had been evinced on board about the propriety of working on Sunday, which had hitherto been touched upon as delicately as possible. All hands being called aft, the writer, from the quarter deck, stated generally the nature of the service, expressing his hopes that every man would feel himself called upon to consider the erection of a lighthouse on the Bell Rock, in every point of view, as a work of necessity and mercy. At the same time it was intimated that if any were of a different opinion, they should be perfectly at liberty to hold their sentiments without the imputation of contumacy or disobedience; the only difference would be in regard to the pay.

Upon stating this much, he stepped into his boat, requesting all who were so disposed to follow him. The sailors, from their habits, found no scruple on this subject, and all of the artificers, though a little tardy, also embarked, excepting four of the masons, who from the beginning mentioned that they would decline working on Sundays. It may here be noticed that throughout the whole of the operations it was observable that the men wrought, if possible, with more keenness upon the Sundays than at other times, from an impression that they were engaged in a work of imperious necessity, which required every possible exertion.

## *CHAPTER V*

## The foundation pit begun. Trial stones landed on the rock.

24TH AUGUST. The operations at this time were entirely directed to the erection of the beacon, in which every man felt an equal interest, as at this critical period the slightest casualty to any of the boats at the rock might have been fatal to himself individually, while it was perhaps peculiar to the writer more immediately to feel for the safety of the whole. Each log or

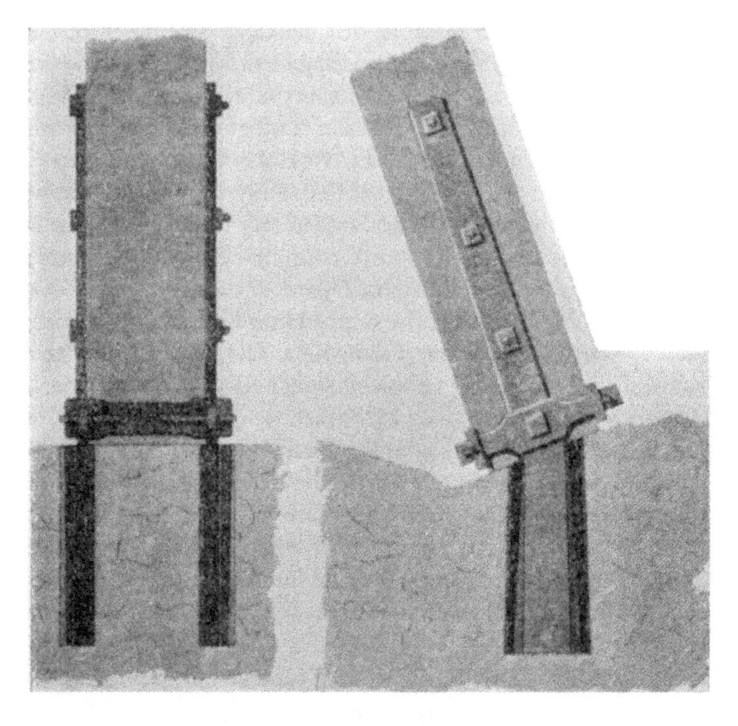

Method of fixing the beams of the beacon to the rock

upright beam of the beacon was to be fixed to the rock by two strong and massive bats or stanchions of iron. These bats for the fixture of the principal and diagonal beams and bracing-chains required fifty-four holes, each measuring two inches in diameter and eighteen inches in depth. The operation of boring or drilling these deep holes in the rock was conducted with great dexterity in the following manner: Three men were attached to each jumper or chisel; one placed himself in a sitting posture, to guide the instrument and give it a turn at each blow of the hammer; he also sponged or cleaned out the hole, and supplied it occasionally with a little water; while the other two, with hammers of sixteen pounds weight, struck the jumper alternately, generally bringing the hammer with a swing round the shoulder, after the manner of blacksmith's work.

There had already been so considerable a progress made in boring and excavating these holes that the writer's hopes of getting the beacon erected this year began to be more and more confirmed, although it was now advancing towards what was considered the latter end of the proper working season at the Bell Rock. The foreman joiner, Mr Francis Watt, was accordingly appointed to attend at the rock today, when the necessary levels were taken for the step or seat of each particular beam of the beacon, that they might be cut to their respective lengths to suit the inequalities of the rock.

25TH AUGUST. The masons and pickmen were employed in boring the bat-holes, and in dressing and preparing the rock between the holes, at the places on which the beams of the beacon-house were to rest. It being now the period of neap-tides, the water only partially left the rock, and some of the men, who were boring on the lower ledges of the site of the beacon, stood knee-deep in water. The situation of the smith today was particularly disagreeable, but his services were at all times indispensable. As the tide did not leave the site of the forge, he stood in the water, and as there was some roughness on the surface, it was with considerable difficulty that, with the assistance of the sailors, he was enabled to preserve alive his fire. While his feet were immersed in water, his face was not only scorched but continually exposed to volumes of smoke, accompanied with sparks from the fire, which were occasionally set up owing to the strength and direction of the wind.

27TH AUGUST. The Smeaton came from Arbroath this afternoon, and made fast to her moorings, having brought letters and newspapers, with parcels of clean linen, &c. for the workmen; who were also made happy by the arrival of three of their comrades from the work-yard ashore. From these men they not only received all the news of the work-yard, but seemed themselves to enjoy great pleasure in communicating whatever they considered to be interesting with regard to the rock. Some also got letters from their friends at a distance, the postage of which, for the men afloat, was always free, so that they corresponded the more readily.

29TH AUGUST. In the course of the night, the wind had shifted from S.E. to S.W., and it blew very hard, being technically termed a *stiff gale*, or rather too much wind for a fishing-boat. It was therefore considered unsafe for the Smeaton to continue at her moorings, and the signal was made for her to sail for Arbroath; she therefore got under way, but although there was a packet of letters for the shore, and the artificers had their memorandums in readiness, yet the floating-light rolled so unmercifully that it would have been at the imminent hazard of staving or dashing a boat to pieces, had it been attempted to put one out. For the present, the Smeaton was obliged to pass at a considerable distance, without being able to communicate with the floating-light.

30TH AUGUST. This being Sunday, the usual ceremony was observed at 12 noon, when the writer read prayers on the quarter-deck. At 3 p.m. all the artificers embarked for the rock, excepting the four men who had declined it last Sunday. Their

View of the rock and foundation-pit
(The men on the right are pumping water from the pit)

places, however, were willingly taken by the three men who came last from the shore, who were happy to get relief from the disagreeable motion of the floating-light upon any terms. The boats reached the rock at half-past 3; but being rather early in the tide, the men rested on their oars till 4 o'clock, and then landed on the different spots as they dried, where they remained till the tide ebbed sufficiently to allow them to commence work. This was the first time the artificers had landed on the rock for five days, owing to the state of the weather and tides, and it was not a little flattering, on this occasion, to see with what eagerness the workmen leaped upon it.

The site of the building having already been carefully traced out with the pick-axe, the artificers this day commenced the excavation of the rock for the foundation or first course of the lighthouse. Four men only were employed at this work, while twelve continued at the site of the beacon-house, at which every possible opportunity was embraced till this essential part of the operations should be completed.

1ST SEPTEMBER. The Smeaton had arrived from Arbroath in the course of the last night. Agreeably to appointment, she had brought off six blocks of granite, for the purpose of making an experiment regarding the landing of the stones on the rock. She also had in tow the praam, or decked boat. This boat, in smooth water, could carry about six or seven tons upon deck.

The writer had looked forward to the trial of landing weighty materials upon the rock as a matter which was to determine an important point in the operations of the Bell Rock Lighthouse, and which could hardly be resolved by any other means than actual trial.

The mode by which the stones were taken out of the Smeaton's hold, and lowered on the praam's deck, will be understood from the illustration. The landing of the materials has been considered one of the most nice and difficult parts of seamanship, and the best informed seamen were unable to say how it might answer, without great risk to the crew, and damage to the stones, and even occasionally losing them between the ship and praam-boat. Both vessels being afloat, and riding in

Method of loading stones on to the praam-boat

the open sea at the distance of about a quarter of a mile from the Bell Rock, their motion was instantly communicated to the landing-gaff, and so to the stone in the tackle. The six blocks of granite having been placed upon the praam's deck, she was towed to a floating-buoy, where she was made fast until the proper time of tide for taking her into one of the creeks of the rock.

The work of the evening tide commenced at a quarter before 5. The sailors having previously decorated the ships and praam-boat with flags, she was towed to the rocks by two boats. The writer having resolved personally to attend the whole progress of this experiment went on board of the praam-boat, when she entered the eastern creek, where the foreman builder, at the head of the artificers, gave three hearty cheers. In the present unprepared state of the machinery and implements upon the rock, the stones, in the present case, were raised with pinches, and pushed ashore upon planks. The whole of this experiment succeeded to the writer's utmost expectation, who was thus led to conclude that the materials might be landed with much more expedition and certainty than he had previously supposed. All hands spontaneously collected to witness the landing of the first stone, which had no sooner touched the rock, than other three cheers were given, and, on this occasion, a glass of rum was served out by the steward.

## *CHAPTER VI*

## The Smeaton goes adrift. Thirty-two men marooned on the rock. A timely rescue.

2ND SEPTEMBER. Soon after the artificers landed they commenced work; but the wind coming to blow hard, the Smeaton's boat and crew, who had brought their complement of eight men to the rock, went off to examine her riding ropes and see that they were in proper order. The boat had no sooner reached the vessel than she went adrift, carrying the boat along with her, and both had got to a considerable distance before this situation of things was observed, everyone being so intent upon his particular duty that the boat had not been seen leaving the rock. By the time that she was got round to make a tack towards the rock, she had drifted at least three miles to leeward, with the praam-boat astern; and having both the wind and tide against her, the writer perceived, with no little anxiety, that she could not possibly return to the rock till long after its being overflowed.

In this perilous predicament, indeed, he found himself placed between hope and despair,—but certainly the latter was by much the most predominant feeling in his mind,—situate upon a sunken rock in the middle of the ocean, which, in the progress of the flood-tide, was to be laid under water to the depth of at least twelve feet in a stormy sea. There were this morning thirty-two persons in all upon the rock, with only two boats, whose complement, even in good weather, did not exceed twenty-four sitters; but to row to the floating-light with so much wind, and in so heavy a sea, a complement of eight men for each boat was as much as could with propriety be attempted, so that, in this way, about one-half of our number was unprovided for.

The unfortunate circumstance of the Smeaton and her boat having drifted was, for a considerable time, only known to the writer and to the landing-master. While the artificers were at work, chiefly in sitting or kneeling postures, excavating the rock, or boring with the jumpers, and while their numerous hammers, and the sound of the smith's anvil continued, the situation of things did not appear so awful. In this state of suspense, with almost certain destruction at hand, the water began to rise upon those who were at work on the lower parts of the sites of the beacon and lighthouse. From the run of the sea upon the rock, the forge fire was also sooner extinguished this morning than usual, and the volumes of smoke having ceased, objects in every direction became visible from all parts of the rock. After having had about three hours' work, the men began to make towards their respective boats for their jackets and stockings, when, to their astonishment, instead of three, they found only two boats, the third being adrift with the Smeaton. Not a word was uttered by any one, but all appeared to be silently calculating their numbers, and looking to each other with evident marks of perplexity depicted in their countenances. The workmen looked steadfastly upon the writer, and turned occasionally towards the vessel, still far to leeward. All this passed in the most perfect silence, and the melancholy solemnity of the group made an impression never to be effaced from his mind.

He was accordingly about to address the artificers on the perilous nature of their circumstances, and to propose that all hands should unstrip their upper clothing when the higher parts of the rock were laid under water; that the seamen should remove every unnecessary weight and encumbrance from the boats; that a specified number of men should go into each boat, and that the remainder should hang by the gunwales, while the boats were to be rowed gently towards the Smeaton, as the course to the Pharos or floating-light lay rather to windward of the rock. But when he attempted to speak, his mouth was so parched that his tongue refused utterance. He then turned to one of the pools on the rock and lapped a little water, which produced immediate relief. But what was his happiness, when, on rising from this unpleasant beverage, some one called out 'A boat, a boat!' and, on looking around, at no great distance a large boat was seen through the haze making towards the rock. This at once enlivened and rejoiced every heart. The timely visitor proved to be James Spink, the Bell Rock pilot, who had come express from Arbroath with letters. Spink had, for some time, seen the Smeaton, and had even supposed, from the state of the weather, that all hands were on board of her, till he approached more nearly and observed people upon the rock; but not supposing that the assistance of his boat was necessary to carry the artificers off the rock, he anchored on the lee-side and began to fish, waiting, as usual, till the letters were sent for, as the pilot-boat was too large and unwieldy for approaching the rock.

Upon this fortunate change of circumstances, sixteen of the artificers were sent, at two trips, in one of the boats, with instructions for Spink to proceed with them to the floating-light. This being accomplished, the remaining sixteen followed in the two boats belonging to the service of the rock. The boats left the rock about 9, but did not reach the vessel till 12 o'clock noon, after a most disagreeable and fatiguing passage of three hours. Everyone was as completely drenched in water as if he had been dragged astern of the boats.

There can be very little doubt that the appearance of James Spink with his boat on this critical occasion was the means of preventing the loss of lives at the rock this morning.

3RD SEPTEMBER. The bell rang this morning at 5 o'clock, but the writer must acknowledge, from the circumstances of yesterday, that its sound was extremely unwelcome. This appears also to have been the feeling of the artificers, for when they came to be mustered, out of twenty-six, only eight, besides the foreman and seamen, appeared upon deck to accompany the writer to the rock. Such are the baneful effects of anything like misfortune or accident connected with a work of this description. The boats reached the rock at 6 a.m., and the eight artificers who landed were employed in clearing out the bat-holes for the beacon-house, and had a very prosperous tide of four hours' work, being the longest yet experienced by half an hour.

The boats left the rock again at 10 o'clock, and the weather having cleared up as we drew near the vessel, the eighteen artificers who had remained on board were observed upon deck; but as the boats approached, they sought their way below, being quite ashamed of their conduct. This was the only instance of refusal to go to the rock which occurred during the whole progress of the work, excepting that of the four men who declined working upon Sunday. It may here be mentioned, much to the credit of these four men, that they stood foremost in embarking for the rock this morning.

## *CHAPTER VII*

# Rough weather. Riding out the gale on the floating-light. A terrifying experience.

5TH SEPTEMBER. The work could not be carried on by torch-light with any degree of safety till the beacon was erected, and the tide fell rather late for landing this evening. Although the weather would have admitted of this, yet the swell of the sea, observable in the morning, still continued to increase. It was so far fortunate that a landing was not attempted, for at 8 o'clock the wind shifted to E.S.E. and at 10 it had become a hard gale.

6TH SEPTEMBER. During the last night there was little rest on board of the Pharos, and daylight, though anxiously wished for, brought no relief, as the gale continued with unabated violence. The sea struck so hard upon the vessel's bows that it rose in great quantities, or in 'green seas', as the sailors termed it, which were carried by the wind as far aft as the quarter-deck, and not infrequently over the stern of the ship altogether. It fell occasionally so heavily on the skylight of the writer's cabin, though so far aft as to be within five feet of the helm, that the glass was broken to pieces before the dead-light could be got into its place, so that the water poured down in great quantities. In shutting out the water, the admission of light was prevented, and in the morning all continued in the most comfortless state of darkness. About 10 o'clock a.m., the wind shifted to N.E., and blew, if possible, harder than before, and it was accompanied by a much heavier swell of sea. In this state things remained during the whole day. Every sea which struck the vessel—and the seas followed each other in close succession—caused her to shake, and all on board occasionally to tremble. At each of these strokes of the sea, the rolling and pitching of the vessel ceased for a time, and her motion was felt as if she had either broke adrift before the wind, or were in the act of sinking; but when another sea came, she ranged up against it with great force, and this became the regular intimation of our being still riding at anchor.

About 11 o'clock, the writer with some difficulty got out of bed, but in attempting to dress, he was thrown twice upon the floor, at the opposite side of the cabin. In an undressed state, he made shift to get about half way up the companion-stairs, with an intention to observe the state of the sea, and of the ship upon deck, but he no sooner looked over the companion than a heavy sea struck the vessel, which fell on the quarter-deck, and rushed down stairs into the officers' cabin in so considerable a quantity that it was found necessary to lift one of the scuttles in the floor, to let the water into the limbers of the ship, as it dashed from side to side in such a manner as to run into the lower tier of beds. Having been foiled in this attempt, and being completely wetted, he again got below and went to bed. The writer even found himself so much tossed about that it became necessary, in some measure, to shut himself in bed in order to avoid being thrown on to the floor. On deck the most stormy aspect presented itself, while below all was wet and comfortless.

About 2 o'clock p.m. a great alarm was given through the ship from the effects of a very heavy sea which struck her, and almost filled the waist, pouring down into the berths below through every chink and crevice of the hatches and sky-lights. From the motion of the vessel being thus suddenly deadened or checked, and from the flowing in of the water above, it is believed there was not an individual on board who did not think, at the moment, that the vessel had foundered, and was in the act of sinking. The writer could withstand this no longer, and as soon as she again began to range to the sea, he determined to make another effort to get upon deck. In the first instance, however, he groped his way in darkness from his own cabin through the berths of the officers, where all was quietness. He next entered the galley and other compartments occupied by the artificers: here also all was shut up in darkness, the fire having been drowned out in the early part of the gale. Several of the artificers were employed in prayer, repeating psalms and other devotional exercises in a full tone of voice; others protesting that if they should fortunately get once more on shore, no one should ever see them afloat again. With the assistance of the landing-master the writer made his way, holding on step by step, among the numerous impediments which lay in the way. Such was the creaking noise of the bulk-heads or partitions, the dashing of the water, and the whistling noise of the winds, that it was hardly possible to break in upon such a confusion of sounds. The next berth in succession, moving forward in the ship, was that allotted for the seamen. Here the scene was considerably different. Having reached the middle of this darksome berth without its inmates being aware of any intrusion, the writer had the consolation of remarking that although they talked of bad weather and the cross accidents of the sea, yet the conversation was carried on in that sort of tone and manner which bespoke an ease and composure of mind highly creditable to them and pleasing to him. The writer immediately accosted the seamen about the state of the ship. To these inquiries they replied that the vessel being light, and having but little hold of the water, no top rigging, with excellent ground-tackle, and everything being fresh and new, they felt perfect confidence in their situation.

The writer, therefore, made the best of his way aft, and on a second attempt to look out, he succeeded, and saw indeed an astonishing sight. The seas, or waves, appeared to be ten or fifteen feet in height of unbroken water, and every approaching billow seemed as if it would overwhelm our vessel, but she continued to rise upon the waves and to fall between the seas in a very wonderful manner. It seemed to be only those seas which caught her in the act of rising which struck her with so much violence and threw such quantities of water aft. On deck there was only one solitary individual looking out, to give the alarm in the event of the ship breaking from her moorings. When the writer looked up, he appeared to smile, which afforded a further symptom of the confidence of the crew in their ship.

By this time it was about 3 o'clock in the afternoon, and the gale, which had now continued with unabated force for 27 hours, had not the least appearance of going off. About 6 o'clock in the evening the ship's company was heard moving upon deck, which on the present occasion was rather the cause of alarm. The writer accordingly rang his bell to know what was the matter, when he was informed by the steward that the weather looked considerably better, and that the men upon deck were endeavouring to ship the smoke-funnel of the galley, that the people might get some meat. This was a more favourable account than had been anticipated. During the last twenty-one hours he himself had not only had nothing to eat, but he had almost never passed a thought on the subject. Upon the mention of a change of weather, he sent the steward to learn how the artificers felt, and on his return he stated that they now seemed to be all very happy, since the cook had begun to light the galley-fire, and make preparations for the suet-pudding of Sunday, which was the only dish to be attempted for the mess, from the ease with which it could both be cooked and served up.

By 9 o'clock all hands had been refreshed by the exertions of the cook and steward, and were happy in the prospect of the worst of the gale being over. Although the previous night had been a very restless one, it had not the effect of inducing repose in the writer's berth on the succeeding night; for having been so much tossed about in bed during the last thirty hours, he found no easy spot to turn to, and his body was all sore to the touch, which ill accorded with the unyielding materials with which his bed-place was surrounded.

This morning, about 8 o'clock, the writer was agreeably surprised to see the scuttle of his cabin sky-light removed, and the bright rays of the sun admitted. Although the ship continued to roll excessively, and the sea was still running very high, yet the ordinary business on board seemed to be going forward on deck. It was impossible to steady a telescope, so as to look minutely at the progress of the waves and trace their breach upon the Bell Rock, but the height to which the cross-running waves rose in sprays when they met each other was truly grand, and the continued roar and noise of the sea was very perceptible to the ear. To estimate the height of the sprays at forty or fifty feet would surely be within the mark. Those of the workmen who were not much afflicted with sea-sickness came upon deck, and the wetness below being dried up, the cabins were again brought into a habitable state. Every one seemed to meet as if after a long absence, congratulating his neighbour upon the return of good weather.

## CHAPTER VIII

# Work resumed at the rock. The derrick erected.

14TH SEPTEMBER. The Smeaton having returned from Arbroath this morning, the writer went on board of her, carrying with him all the artificers. At 6 an attempt was made to land, but the sea ran so heavily, and the breakers rushed with such fury in every direction, that after rowing all around the rock the boats were obliged to return without success. It deserves remark, however, that this was the first attempt to land this season in which it had been found impracticable after actually embarking in the boats.

15TH SEPTEMBER. This morning at 5 a.m., the bell rang as a signal for landing upon the rock, a sound which, after a lapse of ten days, it is believed was welcomed by everyone on board. There being a heavy breach of sea at the eastern creek, we landed, though not without difficulty, on the western side, everyone seeming more eager than another to get upon the rock, and never did hungry men sit down to a hearty meal with more appetite than the artificers began to pick the dulse from the rocks. This marine plant had the effect of reviving the sickly, and seemed to be no less relished by those who were more hardy.

While the water was ebbing, and the men were roaming in quest of their favourite morsel, the writer was examining the effects of the storm upon the forge and loose apparatus left upon the rock. The six large blocks of granite which had been landed, by way of experiment, on the 1st instant, were now removed from their places, and, by the force of the sea, thrown over a rising ledge into a hole at a distance of twelve or fifteen paces from the place on which they had been landed. This was a pretty good evidence both of the violence of the storm and the agitation of the sea upon the rock. The safety of the smith's forge was always an object of essential regard. The ash-pan of the hearth or fire-place, with its weighty cast-iron back, had been washed from their places of supposed security; the chains of attachment had been broken, and these ponderous articles were found at a very considerable distance in a hole on the western side of the rock; while the tools and picks of the Aberdeen masons were scattered about in every direction. It is, however, remarkable that not a single article was ultimately lost.

This being the night on which the floating-light was advertised to be lighted, it was accordingly exhibited, to the great joy of every one. The event of lighting up this ship was ushered in with three hearty cheers, and a dram was served out to all hands.

16TH SEPTEMBER. The writer was made happy today by the return of the lighthouse yacht from a voyage to the Northern Lighthouses. Having immediately removed on board of this fine vessel of eighty-one tons register, the artificers gladly followed, for, though they found themselves more pinched for accommodation on board of the yacht, and still more so in the Smeaton, yet they greatly preferred either of these to the Pharos or floating-light, on account of her rolling motion, though in all respects fitted up for their convenience.

The writer called them to the quarter-deck and informed them that having been one month afloat, in terms of their agreement, they were now at liberty to return to the work-yard at Arbroath if they preferred this to continuing at the Bell Rock. But they replied that in the prospect of soon getting the beacon erected upon the rock, and having made a change from the floating-light, they were now perfectly reconciled to their situation, and would remain afloat till the end of the working season. Of those who had originally come off to the work on the 17th of August, only one man, who was a great martyr to sea-sickness, had returned to the work-yard.

18TH SEPTEMBER. An important occurrence connected with the operations of this season was the arrival of the Smeaton at 4 p.m., having in tow the six principal beams of the beacon-house, together with all the stanchions and other work on board for fixing it on the rock.

In the erection of the beacon at this late period of the season, new difficulties presented themselves. The success of such an undertaking at any season was precarious, because a single day of bad weather occurring before the necessary fixtures could be made might sweep the whole apparatus from the rock. Notwithstanding these difficulties the writer had determined to make the trial, although he could almost have wished, upon looking at the state of the clouds, and the direction of the wind, that the apparatus for the beacon had been still in the work-yard.

19TH SEPTEMBER. The main beams of the beacon were made up in two separate rafts, fixed with bars and bolts of iron. One of these rafts, not being immediately wanted, was left astern of the floating-light, and the other was kept in tow by the Smeaton at the buoy nearest to the rock. The lighthouse yacht rode at another buoy, with all hands on board that could possibly be spared out of the floating-light; including also ten additional men, as carpenters, smiths and sailors, brought off for this operation. The party of artificers and seamen which landed this morning on the Bell Rock counted altogether forty in number. At half-past 8 o'clock a derrick, or mast of thirty feet in height, was erected and properly supported with guy-ropes, for suspending the block for raising the first principal beam of the beacon; and a winch-machine was also bolted down to the rock for working the purchase-tackle. The necessary blocks and tackle were likewise laid to hand and properly arranged. The artificers and seamen were severally allotted in squads to different stations; some were to bring the principal beams to hand, others were to work the tackles, while a third set had the charge of the iron stanchions, bolts, and wedges, so that the whole operation of raising the beams, and fixing them to the rock, might go forward in such a manner that some provision might be made, in every stage of the work, for securing what had been accomplished, in case of a change of weather.

Upon raising the derrick, all hands on the rock spontaneously gave three hearty cheers, as a favourable omen of our future exertions in pointing out more permanently the position of the rock. Even to this single spar of timber, could it be preserved, a drowning man might lay hold. When the Smeaton drifted on the 2nd of this month such a spar would have been sufficient to save us till she could have come to our relief.

## *CHAPTER IX*

## The principal beams of the beacon are set up. Rough weather delays the work.

20TH SEPTEMBER. The wind this morning was variable, but the weather continued extremely favourable for the operations throughout the whole day. At 6 a.m. the boats were in motion, and the raft, consisting of four of the six principal beams of the beacon-house, each measuring about sixteen inches square, and fifty feet in length, was towed to the rock, where it was anchored, that it might ground upon it as the water ebbed. At 7 a.m. the boats of the floating-light, the yacht, and the Smeaton arrived

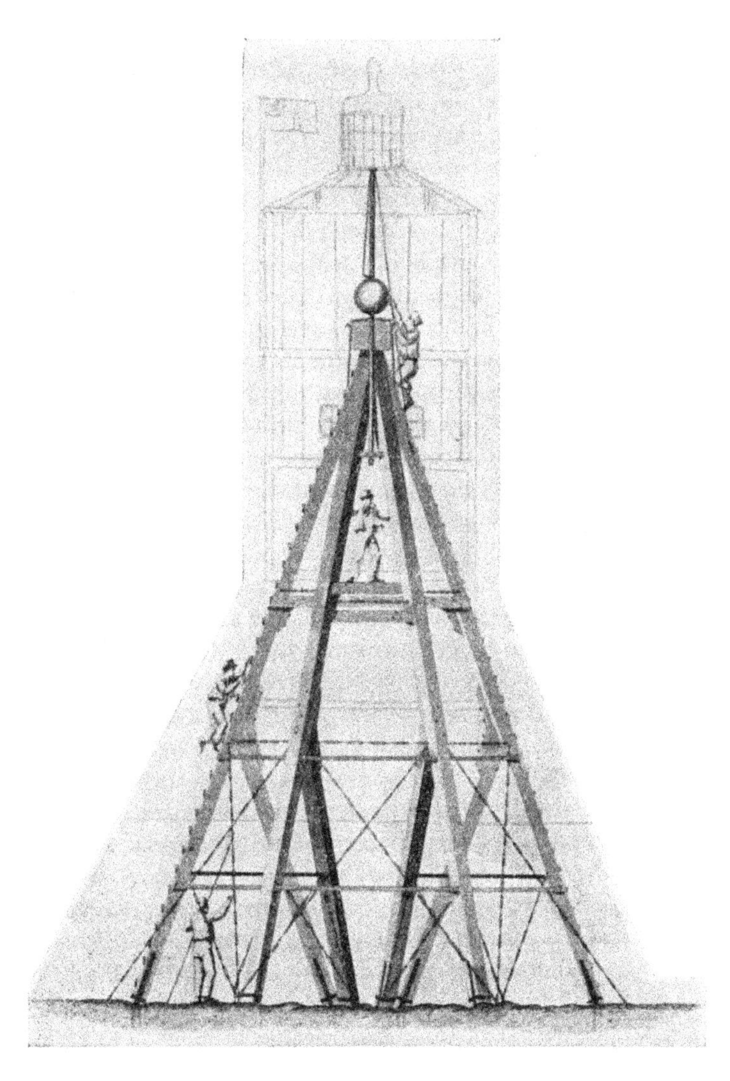

The beacon as completed in 1807
(The faint lines indicate the beacon-house which was added in 1808)

at the rock, when the work immediately commenced. The sailors and artificers, including all hands today, counted no fewer than fifty-two, being perhaps the greatest number of persons ever collected upon the Bell Rock. It was early in the tide when the boats reached the rock, and the men worked a considerable time up to their middle in water, every one being more eager than his neighbour to be useful. Even the four artificers who had hitherto declined working on Sunday were to-day most zealous in their exertions; they had indeed become so convinced of the precarious nature and necessity of the work that they never afterwards absented themselves from the rock on Sunday, when a landing was practicable.

Having made fast a piece of very good new line, at about two thirds from the lower end of one of the beams, the purchase-tackle of the derrick was hooked into the turns of the line, and it was speedily raised, by a number of men on the rock, and by the power of the winch-tackle. When this log was lifted to a sufficient height, its foot, or lower end, was *stepped* into the spot which had been previously prepared for it. Two of the great iron stanchions were then set into their respective holes on each side of the beam, when a rope was passed round them and the beam, to prevent it from slipping till it could be more permanently fixed. The second beam was laid in such a position that when hoisted up its foot slipped into its place, when it was, in like manner, lashed to its great iron stanchions on each side. The first and second beams, being lashed to one another at the top, served as a pair of sheers, from which the purchase-tackle was now suspended for raising the other two beams, which were also speedily got into their places. Having thus got four of the six principal beams set on end, it required a considerable degree of trouble to get their upper ends to fit. Here they formed the apex of a cone, and were all together mortised into a large piece of beechwood, and secured, for the present, with ropes in a temporary manner. During the short period of one tide, all that could further be done for their security was to put a single screw-bolt through the great kneed bats or stanchions on each side of the beams, and screw the nut home. In this manner each beam, with its respective pair of bats, was fixed, besides being strongly bound together with ropes.

While one set of the artificers were employed in this operation, another fixed the great iron stanchions into the rock, into which they were sunk to the depth of about twenty inches. Instead of running the bat-holes full of melted lead, as is common in operations of this kind, but which, in case of friction or movement, is apt to be squeezed out of the holes, all the bats made use of at the Bell Rock were fixed by means of wedges. Several of the artificers were therefore employed in wedging these stanchions first with fir-timber, then with oak, and lastly with iron, driven into spaces left for this purpose between the bats and the rock. These wedges were driven so firmly, that although the stanchions were the only fixture for this wooden house, it had not been found necessary to drive any of the wedges a second time.

In this manner these four principal beams were erected, and left in a pretty secure state. When the first boats left the rock with the artificers employed on the lower part of the work during the flood-tide, the beacon had quite a novel appearance. The beams erected formed a common base of about thirty-three feet meeting at the top, which was about forty-five feet above the rock, and here half a dozen of the artificers were still at work. After clearing the rock, the boats made a stop, when three hearty cheers were given, which were returned with equal good will by those upon the beacon, from the personal interest which every one felt in the prosperity of this work, so intimately connected with his safety.

21ST SEPTEMBER. The weather most fortunately continued favourable for the operations, the wind being westerly, with fresh breezes. The boats landed at half-past 7 a.m., the number of persons on the rock being, as formerly, fifty-two; the work was carried on till half-past 12, making four hours and a half upon the rock. The remaining two principal beams were erected in the course of this tide, which, with the assistance of those set up yesterday, was found to be a very simple operation. In hoisting up the sixth and last log, however, and just when it was about to be canted into its place, the iron hook of the principal purchase-block gave way, and this great beam, measuring fifty feet in length, fell upon the rock with a terrible crash. What is not a little wonderful, although there were fifty-two people engaged round the beacon, is that not one was hurt in the slightest degree by its fall. Another block was immediately hooked in the place of that which had failed, and the beam was got into its place without much delay. The six principal beams of the beacon were thus secured, at least in a temporary manner, in the course of two tides, or in the short space of about eleven hours and a half. Such is the progress that may be made, when active hands and willing minds set properly to work in operations of this kind.

22ND SEPTEMBER. The wind today was due west, and blowing so fresh that the boats had some difficulty in landing thirty-six persons at 8 a.m., who continued on the rock till half-past 12, having had four and a half hours' work. During this tide four of the struts, or supporting beams, were set up, butting against the inside of four of the principal beams.

23RD SEPTEMBER. Landed at half-past 9 this morning, and succeeded in getting up the two remaining supports, and in fixing several of the bracing chains. The Smeaton returned from Arbroath this afternoon, but there was so much sea that she could not be made fast to her moorings; she therefore let go her small bower anchor, in order to get a supply of provisions put on board of the lighthouse yacht, and to receive six of the artificers to carry ashore. But the anchor was no sooner let go than it broke among the rocks, and the vessel was obliged to return to Arbroath, without being able either to deliver the provisions, or take the artificers on board. The lighthouse yacht was also soon obliged to follow her example, as the sea was breaking heavily over her bows. In these circumstances, it was impossible for the writer to divest himself of much anxiety for the fate of the newly erected beacon, which was still but imperfectly fixed to the rock.

25TH SEPTEMBER. The wind still continues at S.W., blowing very hard; at 7 o'clock bore away for the Bell Rock, but finding a heavy sea running on it, were unable to land. The writer, however, had the satisfaction to observe, with his telescope, that everything about the beacon appeared entire, and although the sea had a most frightful appearance, yet it was the opinion of everyone that since the erection of the beacon the Bell Rock was divested of many of its terrors, and, had it been possible to have got the boats hoisted out and manned, it might have even been found practicable to land; the vessel was therefore kept in the track of the rock, till it could be determined if a landing might be effected with the afternoon's tide. The artificers being sea-hardy were quite reconciled to their quarters on board of the lighthouse yacht; but it is believed that hardly any consideration would have induced them again to take up their abode in the floating-light.

## *CHAPTER X*

# The forge moved to the beacon. Another gale. Work finished at the rock for the season. Preparations ashore for next year's work.

26TH SEPTEMBER. At daylight the yacht steered towards the Bell Rock, and at 8 a.m. made fast to her moorings; at 10, all hands, to the amount of thirty, landed, when the writer had the happiness to find that the beacon had withstood the violence of the gale and the heavy breach of sea, everything being found in the same state in which it had been left on the 21st. The artificers were now enabled to work upon the rock throughout the whole day, both at low and high water, but it required the strictest attention to the state of the weather, in case of their being overtaken with a gale, which might prevent the possibility of getting them off the rock.

Two somewhat memorable circumstances in the annals of the Bell Rock attended the operations of this day; one was the removal of Mr James Dove, the foreman smith, with his apparatus, from the rock to the upper part of the beacon, where the forge was now erected on a temporary platform, laid on the cross beams or upper framing. The other was the artificers having dined for the first time upon the rock, their dinner being cooked on board of the yacht, and sent to them by one of the boats. But what afforded the greatest happiness and relief was the removal of the large bellows, which had all along been a source of much trouble and perplexity, by their hampering and incommoding the boat which carried the smiths and their apparatus. The men belonging to that boat were so delighted with this occurrence that while the bellows were in the act of being hoisted up to their new station they gave three such hearty cheers, from below, as astonished and surprised those who were working the tackle on the beacon to such a degree, that, for a moment, they let the rope slip through their hands. Had they not speedily caught hold again, this useful implement might have been dashed to pieces,—which would have been a misfortune of no small import, considering the state of the works at the present crisis.

28TH SEPTEMBER. The joiners and smiths were ten hours upon the rock today, which was the longest period they had hitherto been upon it at any one time. They now had their dinner regularly sent to the beacon, and could continue at work throughout the whole day while the weather was sufficiently moderate to admit of the boats plying to and from the rock. To-day the water did not leave it, and it was now the seventh day since the lowest part of the foundation or site of the lighthouse had been seen.

The beacon being now in a comparative state of security, the Smeaton was left at the rock as a tender, and the writer sailed in the lighthouse yacht this afternoon to inquire into the operations of the workyard at Arbroath. After setting sail, and looking back upon the Bell Rock, it was quite astonishing to observe the change in the appearance of things which the erection of these beams had produced. To shipping they became an excellent beacon; while they induced the greatest confidence of safety in all who were actively engaged in this work.

29TH SEPTEMBER. This morning was occupied in going over the work-yard with Mr David Logan, clerk of works, who had charge of the hewing department. The first entire course of the building was now partly laid upon the platform: a few stones of the second course, and several of the higher courses, were also in progress.

Having made some further arrangements in the work-yard,

the writer again embarked in the yacht, and sailed for the Bell Rock this forenoon, carrying with him Mr Peter Logan, the foreman builder, and the artificers who had formerly been at the rock. In the early part of this day there was little or no wind, but in the afternoon it came to blow very hard from south by west, and in the evening it had increased to a hard gale.

30TH SEPTEMBER. At midnight we got within a few miles of the light of May, and soon afterwards found smooth water in St Andrew's Bay, where we tacked, or 'stood to and again', as the sailors term it, all night.

This morning the wind shifted to N.E. with moderate breezes. In the course of the forenoon we beat towards the Bell Rock, and sailed round it, when everything appeared to be in good order about the beacon. Having no shelter in St Andrew's Bay with this wind, the yacht stood alternately towards Arbroath and the Bell Rock for the night.

2ND OCTOBER. On carefully examining into the state of things at the Bell Rock, after the late gale, the writer had the satisfaction to find that the principal beams of the beacon, with their diagonal supports, cross-beams and stanchions connecting them to the rock, had not the smallest appearance of working or shifting, as mechanics express it.

3RD OCTOBER. The wind being west today, the weather was very favourable for the operations at the rock, and during the morning and evening tides, with the aid of torch-light, the masons had seven hours' work upon the site of the building. The smiths and joiners, who landed at half-past 6 a.m., did not leave the rock till a quarter past 11 p.m., having been at work with little intermission for sixteen hours and three quarters. When the water left the rock, they were employed at the lower parts of the beacon, and as the tide rose or fell, they shifted the place of their operations. From these exertions, the fixing and securing of the beacon made rapid advancement, as the men were now landed in the morning, and remained throughout the day. But, as a sudden change of weather might have prevented their being taken off at the proper time of tide, a quantity of bread and water was always kept on the beacon.

4TH OCTOBER. The external part of the beacon was now finished, with its supports and bracing-chains, and whatever else was considered necessary for its stability, in so far as the season would permit. A small flag-staff having also been erected to-day, a flag was displayed for the first time from the beacon, by which its perspective effect was greatly improved. On this, as on all like occasions at the Bell Rock, three hearty cheers were given; and the steward served out a dram of rum to all hands, while the lighthouse yacht, Smeaton, and floating-light hoisted their colours in compliment to the erection.

6TH OCTOBER. Everything was now in a prepared state for leaving the rock, and giving up the works afloat for this season, excepting some small matters which would still occupy the smiths and joiners for a few days longer. They accordingly, shifted on board of the Smeaton, while the yacht left the rock for Arbroath with the writer and the remainder of the artificers. But before taking leave, the steward served out a farewell-glass, when three hearty cheers were given, and an earnest wish expressed that everything in the spring of 1808 might be found in the same state of good order as it was now about to be left.

In concluding the account of the first season's work, the writer may observe that he had not at any time previously to his engaging in the Bell Rock works been more than five or six days at sea on a stretch. But on the present occasion he had now been afloat upwards of seven weeks, with the exception of a single day spent in the work-yard. Upon his return to the shore, therefore, after having successfully closed these critical operations, he felt a mixed emotion of happiness and gratitude for so prosperous a termination. The period during which the works had been continued appeared of much longer duration to everyone than it really was, for, upon calculating the actual time spent upon the rock, it amounted to about 180 hours, of which only 133, or about 13½ days of 10 hours each, could be said to have been actively employed. Upon looking back on this result, the writer is astonished at what had been accomplished in so short a period; for besides the erection of the principal beams of the beacon-house, something considerable had also been done towards the preparation of the site of the lighthouse. He cannot, therefore, help thinking that the experience of this season's work at the Bell Rock affords a good example of what may be executed under similar circumstances, when every heart and every hand is anxiously and zealously engaged; for the artificers wrought at the erection of the beacon as for life; or somewhat like men stopping a breach in a wall to keep out an overwhelming flood.

The work-yard at Arbroath, where the stones were collected and hewn, consisted of an enclosed piece of ground extending to about three quarters of an acre. In a central position of this ground a circular platform of masonry was built, on which the stones were laid when dressed, and each course tried and marked before being shipped for the rock. Here the dressed part of the first entire course of the lighthouse was now lying.

The several departments of the Bell Rock works being arranged for the winter months, the sloop Smeaton was appointed to make several trips to the quarries for stones, while the lighthouse yacht, being stationed at Arbroath, was to attend the floating-light, and carry off the artificers to examine the state of the beacon at spring-tides. The writer, having adjusted these matters, returned to Edinburgh on the 4th of December. Here he was employed in preparing the necessary implements, procuring materials, and in other objects connected with the work, which will fall more properly to be noticed in the transactions of the year 1808.

(During much of the past season's work the floating-light had been used as the 'tender' on which the artificers lived when not actually at work on the rock. It was unsatisfactory for several reasons, and for the next year's work the Lighthouse Board provided a vessel of 81 tons specially fitted up as a tender for the Bell Rock works. She was named the 'Sir Joseph Banks' in honour of one who had done much to forward the Lighthouse proposals with the Government.)

## *CHAPTER XI*

## Preparations for landing the stones at the rock. The masons at work ashore. The rock visited. All well after the winter.

The site of the lighthouse being in a central position on the rock, it became necessary to make some provision for conveying the large blocks of stone speedily from the respective landing-places to the site of the building. In ordinary situations the most obvious method would have been to clear away the inequalities of the rock; but here, from the lowness of its position in the water, such an operation would have been extremely tedious and difficult. Instead, therefore, of quarrying the rock, the writer found that the most advisable process would be to lay cast-iron railways round the site of the lighthouse, projecting to the several landing-places, on which waggons could easily be wheeled in all directions.

Connected with the cast-iron railways, preparations were also made at the eastern landing-place for lifting the stones by means of cranes or other machinery from the praam-boats, and laying them upon the waggons to be conveyed to the building.

As the whole of the stones of each course or tier of this

building were connected or let into one another by a system of dovetails diverging from the centre to the circumference, each particular stone required to be cut with accuracy to fit its precise place in the building, and it became a very considerable operation to prepare the necessary moulds or patterns for the respective courses. When, therefore, the thickness was ascertained to which a lot of these stones would admit being dressed, a plan of the particular course was first drawn upon paper by

Method of landing stones on the rock

the Clerk of Works, and a certain part of the course was then enlarged to the full size upon a platform of polished pavement. From this enlarged draught Mr James Slight, the principal mould-maker, took his dimensions in making the moulds of the full size of the ground-plan of each stone, on which were marked the necessary directions for the stone cutter. These moulds being made with great precision, were carefully marked and numbered with oil paint, according to the positions which the respective stones were to occupy.

On the writer's visit to Arbroath in the end of March, he was anxious to land upon the Bell Rock, to ascertain the precise state of the beacon after the storms of the winter, that he might be enabled to judge of the propriety of converting it into a habitable place for the artificers during the working season. He accordingly sailed from Arbroath on the 30th of March, at 1 a.m., in the lighthouse yacht. It was now unfortunately too late

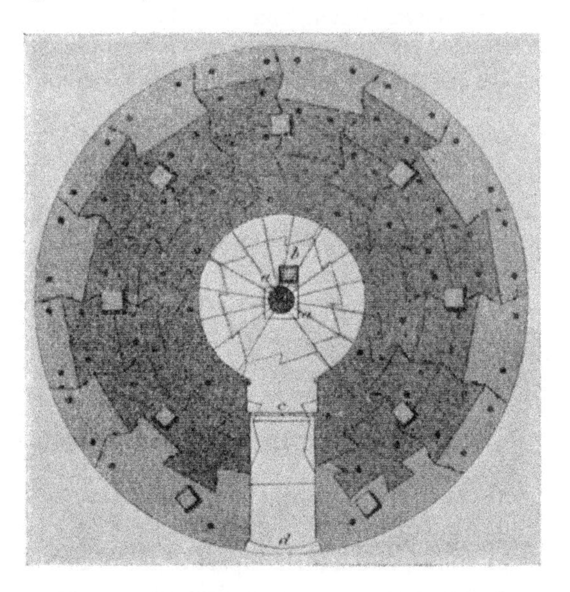

One of the courses of stones, showing how the blocks were dovetailed into one another

in the tide for landing upon the rock this morning; and it became necessary to cruise about till the following day, there being at this season only one tide with daylight.

At daybreak on the following morning, the lighthouse yacht, attended by a boat from the floating-light, again stood towards the Bell Rock. At half-past 7, the sea ran with such force upon the rock that it seemed doubtful if a landing could be effected. At half-past 8, when it was fairly above water, the writer took his place in the floating-light's boat with the artificers, while the yacht's boat followed, according to the general rule of having two boats afloat in landing expeditions of this kind, so that in case of accident to one boat, the other might assist. Watching what the sailors term a *smooth*, we caught a favourable opportunity, and in a very dexterous manner the boats were rowed between the two seas, and made a favourable landing at the western creek. Upon narrowly examining all the parts of the beacon, the writer had the satisfaction of finding

Patterns for the stones of one course

that there was not the least appearance of working or shifting at any of the joints or places of connection; and, excepting the loosening of the bracing-chains, everything was found in the same entire state in which it had been left in the month of October. This, in the estimation of the writer, was a matter of no small importance to the future success of the work. He, from that moment, saw the practicability and propriety of fitting up the beacon, not only as a place of refuge in case of accident to the boats in landing, but as a residence for the artificers during the working months.

After, with some difficulty, getting off the beacon, a proper time was again watched, and, by active rowing, the boats soon cleared the rock in safety, though not without shipping two or three pretty heavy seas. About 12 noon the lighthouse yacht bore away, and at 7 in the evening she reached the Bay of Arbroath, where the writer landed about 8 p.m., and on the following day returned to Edinburgh.

## *CHAPTER XII*

## The season's work begun at the rock. The mortar gallery erected. Busy times at the rock.

25TH MAY. On the 25th the writer embarked at Arbroath, on board of the Sir Joseph Banks, for the Bell Rock, accompanied by Mr Logan senior, foreman-builder, with twelve masons and two smiths, together with thirteen seamen, including the master, mate and steward. The vessel sailed at 3 o'clock p.m. under a salute of three hearty cheers from a great assemblage of people on the quays; but before getting to the rock it was too late for making fast to the moorings that night; and she kept cruising about with the floating-light in view, which proved a great comfort to the seamen, in directing them to tack the ship before she got too near the rock.

26TH MAY. The wind today was at south-east, and though the weather was not very pleasant, yet it was moderate. The bell being accordingly rung, the boats were hoisted out; and, everything being arranged, both boats proceeded in company, and at 8 a.m. they reached the rock. The lighthouse colours were immediately hoisted upon the flag-staff of the beacon, a compliment which was duly returned by the tender and floating-light, when three hearty cheers were given, and a glass of rum was served out to all hands, to drink success to the operations of 1808.

In the evening tide the artificers landed at a quarter past 7, though the sea ran pretty high, and the boats shipped a good deal of water. Being rather early in the tide for working at the site of the building, the time was occupied in getting the smith's forge put in order upon the cross-beams of the beacon, a step of great importance to the future progress and advancement of the work.

28TH MAY. The wind still continued from the eastward, with a heavy swell; and today it was accompanied with foggy weather, and occasional showers of rain. Notwithstanding this, such was the confidence which the erection of the beacon had inspired, that the boats landed the artificers on the rock under very unpromising circumstances, at half-past 8, and they continued at work till half-past 11, being a period of three hours, which was considered a great tide's work in the present low state of the foundation. Three of the masons on board were so afflicted with sea-sickness that they had not been able to take any food for almost three days, and they were literally assisted into the boats this morning by their companions. It was, however, not a little surprising to see how speedily these men revived upon landing on the rock and eating a little dulse. Instead of returning to the tender with the boats, these three men remained on the beacon all day, and had their victuals sent to them along with the smiths'. From Mr Dove, the foreman-smith, they had much sympathy for he preferred remaining on the beacon at all hazards, to be himself relieved from the malady of sea-sickness.

29TH MAY. The wind was from the S.W. today, and the signal-bell rang, as usual, about an hour before the period for landing on the rock. The writer was rather surprised, however, to hear the landing-master repeatedly call, 'All hands for the rock'; and, coming on deck, he was disappointed to find the seamen only in the boats. Upon inquiry it appeared that some misunderstanding had taken place about the wages of the artificers for Sundays. They had preferred wages for seven days statedly, to the former mode of allowing a day for each tide's work on Sunday; as they did not like the appearance of working for double or even treble wages on Sunday, and would rather have it understood that their work on that day arose more from the urgency of the case, than with a view to emolument. This having been judged creditable to their religious feelings, and readily adjusted to their wish, the boats proceeded to the rock, and the work commenced at 9 a.m. The artificers were chiefly employed in removing the iron stanchions or frame-work of the forge, which had last year been fixed on the rock, and which was now set on a temporary scaffold erected for it on the beacon. Having now got two smiths' hearths above the reach of the tide, the work of this department made great progress, both in the sharpening of the numerous picks and irons, and in making bats for fixing the different railway tracks upon the rock.

30TH MAY. Mr Francis Watt commenced, at this tide, with five joiners, to fit up a temporary platform upon the beacon, about twenty-five feet above the highest part of the rock. This platform was to be used as the site of the smith's forge, after the beacon should be fitted up as a barrack; and here also the mortar was to be mixed and prepared for the building. It was accordingly termed the Mortar Gallery.

The landing-master's crew completed the discharging from the Smeaton of the remainder of her cargo of cast-iron rails and timber. It must not here be omitted to notice that the Smeaton took in ballast from the Bell Rock, consisting of the shivers or chips of stone produced by the workmen in preparing the site of the building, which were now accumulated in great quantities on the rock. These the boats loaded, after discharging the iron. The object in carrying off these chips, besides ballasting the vessel, was to get them permanently out of the way, as they were apt to shift about from place to place with every gale of wind; and it often required a considerable time to clear the foundation a second time of this rubbish. The circumstance of ballasting a ship at the Bell Rock afforded great entertainment, especially to the sailors; and it was perhaps with truth remarked that the Smeaton was the first vessel that had ever taken on board ballast at the Bell Rock.

31ST MAY. In the evening the boats went to the Rock, and brought the joiners and smiths, and their sickly companions, on board of the tender. They also brought with them two baskets full of fish, which they had caught at high water from the beacon, reporting at the same time to their comrades that the fish were swimming in such numbers over the rock at high water that it was completely hid from their sight, and nothing seen but the movement of thousands of fish. They were almost exclusively of the species called the Podlie, or young Coal-fish. This discovery, made for the first time today by the workmen, was considered fortunate, as an additional circumstance likely to produce an inclination among the artificers to take up their residence in the beacon, when it came to be fitted up as a barrack.

7TH JUNE. At three o'clock in the morning the ship's bell was rung as the signal for landing at the rock. When the landing was to be made before breakfast, it was customary to give each of the artificers and seamen a dram and a biscuit, and coffee was prepared by the steward for the cabins. Exactly at four o'clock the whole party landed from three boats.

Having now so considerable a party of workmen and sailors on the rock, it may be proper here to notice how their labours were directed. Preparations having been made last month for the erection of a second forge upon the beacon, the smiths commenced their operations both upon the lower and higher platforms, where forges had been erected. They were employed in sharpening the picks and irons for the masons, and in making bats and other apparatus of various descriptions connected with the fitting of the railways. The landing-master's crew were occupied in assisting the mill-wrights in laying the railways to hand. Sailors, of all other descriptions of men, are the most accommodating in the use of their hands. They worked freely with the boring irons, and assisted in all the operations of the railways, acting by turns as boatmen, seamen, and artificers. We had no such character on the Bell Rock as the common labourer. All the operations of this department were cheerfully undertaken by the seamen, who, both on the rock and on ship-board, were the inseparable companions of every work connected with the erection of the Bell Rock Lighthouse. It will naturally be supposed that about twenty-five masons, occupied with their picks in executing and preparing the foundation of the lighthouse, in the course of a tide of about three hours would make a considerable impression upon an area even of forty-two feet in diameter. But in proportion as the foundation was deepened, the rock was found to be much more hard and difficult to work, while the baling and pumping of water became much more troublesome. A joiner was kept almost constantly employed in fitting the picks to their handles, which, as well as the points of the irons, were very frequently broken. At 8 o'clock the water overflowed the site of the building, and the boats left the rock with all hands for breakfast. Several of the artificers would willingly have remained upon the beacon to avoid the rolling motion and sickness incident to the ship; yet, being all wetted, and those especially who were employed in excavating the site of the lighthouse and railways being completely bespattered with the chips from the rock, the whole party embarked in the boats. Such as chose were at liberty to return to the beacon with the smiths after breakfast.

## *CHAPTER XIII*

## Appearance of the works. The foundation-stone landed and laid. The foundation-course completed.

The Bell Rock this morning presented by far the most busy and active appearance it had exhibited since the erection of the beacon. The surface of the rock was crowded with men, the two forges flaming, the one above the other, upon the beacon, while the anvils thundered with the rebounding noise of their wooden supports, and formed a curious contrast with the occasional clamour of the surges. The wind was westerly today, and the weather being extremely agreeable, as soon after breakfast as the tide had sufficiently overflowed the rock to float the boats over it, the smiths, with a number of the artificers, returned to the beacon, carrying their fishing-tackle along with them. In the course of the forenoon, the beacon exhibited a still more extraordinary appearance than the rock had done in the morning. The sea being smooth, it seemed to be afloat upon the water, with a number of men supporting themselves in all the variety of attitude and position; while from the upper part of this wooden house, the volumes of smoke which ascended from the forges gave the whole a very curious and fanciful appearance.

To the distant shipping, the appearance of things at night on the Bell Rock, when the work was going forward, must have been very remarkable, especially to those who were strangers to the operations. Mr John Reid, principal light-keeper, who also acted as master of the floating-light during the working months at the rock, described the appearance of the numerous lights situate so low in the water, when seen at the distance of two or three miles, as putting him in mind of Milton's description of the fiends in the lower regions; adding, 'for it seems greatly to surpass Will-o'-the-Wisp, or any of those earthly spectres of which we have so often heard'.

7TH JULY. The landing-master's bell rang this morning about 4 o'clock, and at 5 the boats landed the artificers, when the pumps and buckets were set to work to clear the foundation-pit of water. At half-past 5, the foundation being cleared, the work commenced on the site of the building. But from the moment of landing, the squad of joiners and mill-wrights was at work upon the higher parts of the rock, in laying the railways, while the anvils of the smiths resounded on the beacon, and such columns of smoke ascended from the forges, that they were often mistaken by strangers at a distance for a ship on fire.

The foundation-pit now assumed the appearance of a great platform, and the late tides had been so favourable that it became apparent that the first course, consisting of a few irregular and detached stones for making up certain inequalities in the interior parts of the site of the building, might be laid in the course of the present spring-tides. Having been enabled to-day to get the dimensions of the foundation or first stone accurately taken, a mould was made of its figure, when the writer left the rock, after the tide's work of this morning, in a fast rowing boat for Arbroath. Upon landing, two men were immediately set to work upon one of the blocks from Mylnefield quarry, which was prepared in the course of the following day, as the stone-cutters relieved each other, and worked both night and day, so that it was sent off in one of the stone-lighters without delay.

9TH JULY. The site of the foundation-stone was very difficult to work, from its depth in the rock, but being now nearly prepared, it formed a very agreeable kind of pastime at high-water for all hands to land the stone itself upon the rock. The landing-master's crew and artificers accordingly entered with great spirit into this operation. The stone was placed upon the deck of the Hedderwick praam-boat, which had just been brought from Leith, and was decorated with colours for the occasion. Flags were also displayed from the shipping in the offing, and upon the beacon. Here the writer took his station with the greater part of the artificers, who supported themselves in every possible position while the boats towed the praam from her moorings, and brought her immediately over the site of the building, where her grappling anchors were let go. The stone was then lifted off the deck by a tackle hooked into a lewis-bat inserted into it; when it was gently lowered into the water and grounded on the site of the building, amidst the cheering acclamations of about sixty persons.

10TH JULY. The wind today was variable, with gentle breezes varying from S.E. to N.E.; and everything being in a state of preparation for laying the foundation-stone, which had yesterday been landed with so much eclat, the sailors again displayed their flags at all points, and a cheerful happiness was discernible in every countenance. At half-past 8 the boats landed the artificers, and, the weather being remarkably fine, as many of the crews of the floating-light, the tender and the Smeaton as could be spared from their respective ships landed this morning, to witness the long-wished-for ceremony of laying the first stone of the lighthouse.

At 11 o'clock, the foundation-stone was laid to hand. It was of a square form containing about 20 cubic feet, and had the figures or date of 1808 simply cut upon it with a chisel. A derrick or spar of timber having been erected at the edge of the hole and guyed with ropes, the stone was then hooked to the tackle and lowered into its place, when the writer, attended by his assistants Mr Peter Logan, Mr Francis Watt and Mr James Wilson, applied the square, the level, and the mallet, and pronounced the following benediction: 'May the Great Architect of the Universe complete and bless this building', on which three hearty cheers were given, and success to the future operations was drunk with the greatest enthusiasm.

14TH JULY. The work now put on a very promising appearance. The first stone had been laid, and the levelling of the site of the building was in such a state as to afford every prospect of being able to commence the building of the first entire course after a few good tides. The *reach* of the railways from the site of the building to the eastern landing-place was also in a state of great forwardness, and the other parts of the apparatus being now in readiness, there was every prospect of making rapid progress after the foundation-course was laid, and building operations were fairly begun.

26TH JULY. The weather being moderate, the boats landed again in the evening at a quarter past 10, and left off at midnight, having had altogether four hours and three quarters' of low-water work today, when the last of the eighteen detached pieces of stone forming the foundation-course were laid. The several holes or cavities in it, varying in depth from six to eighteen inches, had now been built up with stones exactly cut and fitted to their respective places, which brought the whole surface to a uniform level.

In leaving the rock this evening, everything, after the

torches were extinguished, had the same dismal appearance as last night, but so perfectly acquainted were the landing-master

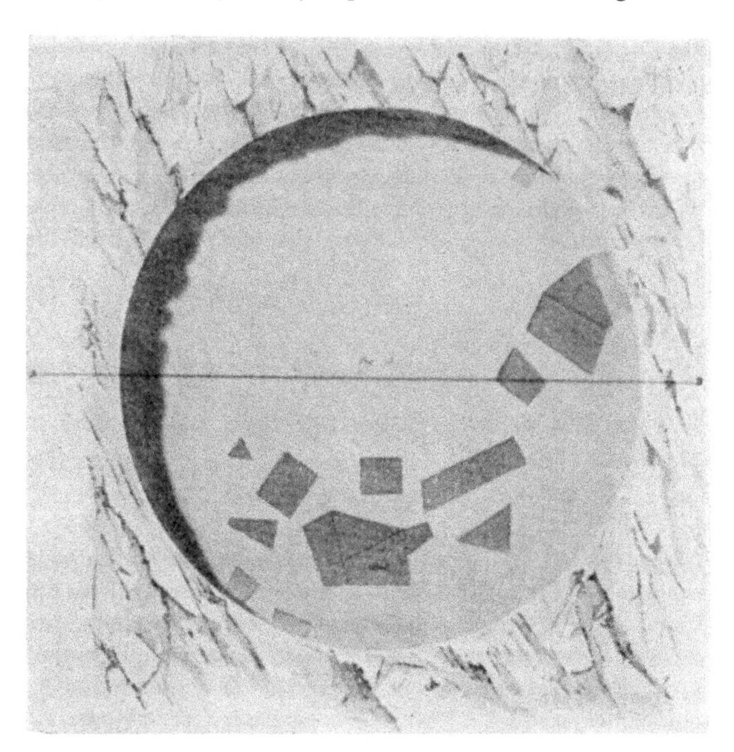

Plan of the foundation-pit and the first or imperfect course, showing the stones which were put in to level up the surface of the rock. (The foundation-stone is marked "1808")

and his crew with the position of things at the rock, that comparatively little inconvenience was experienced on these occasions, when the weather was moderate: such is the effect of habit, even in the most unpleasant situations. If, for example, it had been proposed to a person accustomed to a city life at once to take up his quarters off a sunken reef, and land upon it in boats at all hours of the night, the proposition must have appeared quite impracticable and extravagant; but this practice coming progressively upon the artificers, it was ultimately undertaken with the greatest alacrity. Notwithstanding this, however, it must be acknowledged that it was not till after much labour and peril, and many an anxious hour, that the writer is enabled to state that the site of the Bell Rock Lighthouse was fully prepared for the first entire course of the building.

## *CHAPTER XIV*

## The second and third courses laid. A seaman is drowned. The laying of the fourth course finishes the work of the season.

28TH JULY. The sloop Smeaton had loaded the first cargo of cut stone at Arbroath for the lighthouse, consisting of twenty blocks of the first entire course, and had last night come to her moorings; and this morning the praam-boats were employed in landing her cargo upon the rock. The artificers having landed at 9 a.m., the foundation was cleared of water by 10, when the masons made preparations for commencing the building operations. Having had two hours and three quarters' work, they left the rock, after laying the blocks of stone which had been landed in a compact and regular manner upon the site of the building.

Stones laid at the depth of about 14 feet under high-water mark required more than merely laying them on their respective beds, and trusting to their own gravity. For this purpose nothing seemed to be so well adapted as the oaken trenails which Mr Smeaton used in the erection of the Eddystone Lighthouse. Two jumper-holes, of an inch and a half in diameter, had accordingly been drilled through each stone, and were continued or perforated to the depth of six inches into the rock or course immediately below. This became the most tedious part of the building operation. When the oaken trenail was inserted into the hole, it had a saw-draught across the lower end, into which a small wedge was inserted: and when driven home, it became quite firm. The trenail was then cut flush with the upper bed of the stone, and split with a chisel, when another wooden wedge was inserted and driven into the upper end of the trenail. Nor was this all, for two pairs of oaken wedges were also driven gently into the perpendicular joints, prior to grouting them with mortar.

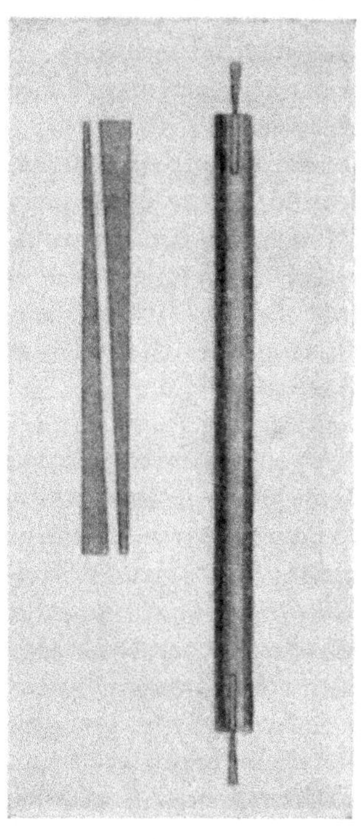

Oaken wedges and trenails

From Saturday the 6th August till Wednesday the 10th inclusive, the weather and tides were favourable, which afforded an opportunity of landing both with the morning and evening tides, and in the course of these five days twenty-six hours' work were obtained, and ninety-two stones were laid.

12TH AUGUST. The artificers landed this morning at half-past 10, and after an hour and a half's work, eight stones were laid, which completed the first entire course of the building, consisting of 123 blocks, the last of which was laid with three hearty cheers. Immediately after this tide the tender left the rock for Arbroath, with all hands on board; and having a fine breeze at south, she got into the harbour at half-past 6 p.m., to wait the return of the spring-tides.

Those on board felt not a little happy when the ship, which, on her passage, had been decorated with colours intimating that the first entire course was laid, was received with cheering from the workmen ashore, and the inhabitants of Arbroath.

27TH AUGUST. The weather having been extremely favourable, regular tides' work were got both morning and evening, so that the second entire course, containing 136 stones in number, and 152 tons' weight, was laid in the course of seven tides; the sloop Smeaton having been kept constantly plying between the Bell Rock and Arbroath, where, on her arrival, she was immediately loaded, whether by night or day.

On completing the laying of the second entire course, the lighthouse began to assume the appearance and form of a building; for, although still under a part of the excavated rock, it was nevertheless 4 feet above the level of the lower bed of the foundation-stone,—a consideration which was highly gratifying to those immediately connected with the work. Having successfully completed this course, the writer sailed with the Smeaton for Arbroath, accompanied by such of the artificers as had been employed in building, and leaving the tender at the Rock with the mill-wrights, joiners, smiths, and masons, who worked at the railways, and at preparing the upper part of the beacon as a barrack.

18TH SEPTEMBER. The artificers landed this morning at 5 o'clock, and continued at work till a quarter past 8. The railways being now in a pretty complete state, and a further supply of stones having been brought to the rock, the landing-master got 21 blocks conveyed from the eastern wharf to the building. In the same manner, with the evening tide, 10 stones were landed, and the work continued from half-past 5 to half-past 8, having had six hours and a quarter's work today, during which no fewer than 31 stones were laid.

21ST SEPTEMBER. Today the wind was at S.W., blowing a fresh gale, and it was not expected that the Smeaton could have possibly returned from Arbroath with the remaining stones of the course in hand, consisting of 17 blocks, with which, because of advanced period of the season and the boisterous state of the weather, it was proposed to terminate the building for this year. The Smeaton, however, got to Arbroath last night at a late hour; and Mr Lachlan Kennedy, Engineer's clerk,—whose department it was to attend to the dispatch of the vessels,—with that promptitude and zeal in the service which uniformly marked all his transactions, called the artificers in the work-yard barrack at midnight, when they commenced, with torch-light, to cart the stones to the quay, and had loaded the Smeaton by half-past 2 a.m., so that she saved tide out of the harbour, and at half-past 6 got to her moorings at the rock.

Mr Thomas Macurich, mate of the Smeaton, and James Scott, one of the crew, a young man about 18 years of age, immediately went into their boat to make fast a hawser to the ring in the top of the floating-buoy of the moorings, and were forthwith to proceed to land their cargo, so much wanted at the rock. The tides at this period were very strong, and the mooring-chain when sweeping the ground had caught hold of a rock or piece of wreck, by which the chain was so shortened that when the tide flowed, the buoy got almost under water, and little more than the ring appeared at the surface. When Macurich and Scott were in the act of making the hawser fast to the ring, the chain got suddenly disentangled at the bottom, and this large buoy vaulted or sprang up with such force that it upset the boat, which instantly filled with water. Mr Macurich, with much exertion, succeeded in getting hold of the boat's gunwale, still above the surface of the water, and by this means was saved; but the young man Scott was unfortunately drowned. He had, in all probability, been struck about the head by the ring of the buoy, for although surrounded with the oars and the thwarts of the boat which floated near him, yet he seemed entirely to want the power of availing himself of such assistance, and appeared to be quite insensible, while Pool, the master of the Smeaton, called loudly to him: and, before assistance could be got from the tender, he was carried away by the strength of the current, and disappeared! A signal of distress was immediately hoisted, when one of the boats of the landing-master's crew instantly attended to Macurich's safety, and picked him up in a very exhausted state, but he happily soon recovered.

The young man Scott was a great favourite in the service, having had something uncommonly mild and complaisant in his manner; and his loss was therefore universally regretted. The circumstances of his case were also peculiarly distressing to his mother, as her husband, who was a seamen, had for three years past been confined to a French prison, and the deceased was the chief support of the family. In order in some measure to make up the loss to the poor woman for the monthly aliment regularly allowed her by her late son, it was suggested that a younger boy, a brother of the deceased, might be taken into the service. This appeared to be rather a delicate proposition, but it was left to the landing-master to arrange according to circumstances: such was the resignation, and at the same time the spirit, of the poor woman, that she readily accepted the proposal, and in a few days the younger Scott was actually afloat in the place of his brother.

At 6 p.m. the artificers landed, and continued at work till half-past 10, when the remaining seventeen stones were laid, which completed the third entire course, or fourth of the lighthouse, with which the building operations were closed for this season.

The works at the rock in September 1808

## OPERATIONS OF 1809

(The winter was spent in continuing the preparation of the stone at Arbroath, and by March 1809 all the courses up to the thirteenth had been made ready. Great difficulty had been experienced in obtaining enough blocks of granite sufficiently large for the work.

During the spring the rock was several times visited by parties of workmen.

An additional vessel, the sloop, Patriot, was fitted up to assist the Smeaton in conveying material to the rock.)

### *CHAPTER XV*

# The third season's building begun. The beacon-house prepared. Eleven men left on the beacon during heavy weather. Their rescue.

The several tides' work which had been got upon the rock this season, had enabled the artificers to refit the damage which the railways had sustained during the winter months, and to make further progress with the great circular track round the building, which measured fifty-five feet in diameter; but, as yet, the western reach had made but little advancement. The fitting up of the temporary residence on the higher part of the beacon began to make some more habitable-like appearance; the joistings for the respective floors were laid, and a few of the upright spars of the framing had also been set up. This work continued to create much interest with every one connected with the operations, as its completion was to relieve those affected with the sea-sickness, and the whole troop from the continual plague of boating to and from the rock by day and night.

23RD MAY. At 5 p.m., the writer embarked with Mr Peter Logan the building-foreman, Captain Wilson the landing-master, and fifteen masons, and sailed for the Bell Rock with the first cargo of stones for this season's operations.

24TH MAY. At 6 a.m. Mr Watt, who conducted the operations of the railways and beacon-house, had landed with nine artificers. At half-past 1 p.m. Mr Peter Logan had also landed with fifteen masons, and immediately proceeded to set up the crane, which still lay lashed to the building. The masons were chiefly employed during this tide in clearing the upper course of the building from sea-weed, of which, since the month of September, it had acquired a thick coating.

27TH MAY. The crane having been raised, and the necessary preparations made for beginning the building for the season, five stones of the fifth course were landed and laid.

31ST MAY. The masons laid 13 stones today, which the seamen had landed together with other building materials. In the morning the snow showers were so thick that it was with difficulty that the landing-master, who always steered the leading-boat, could make his way to the rock through the drift. But at the Bell Rock, neither snow, nor rain, nor fog, nor wind, retarded the progress of the work, if unaccompanied by a heavy swell or breach of the sea.

1ST JUNE. This morning, at a quarter past 8, the artificers were landed as usual, and after three hours and three quarters' work 5 stones were laid, the greater part of this tide having been taken up in completing the boring and trenailing of the stones formerly laid. At noon the writer, with the seamen and artificers, proceeded to the tender, leaving on the beacon the joiners, and several of these who were troubled with sea-sickness, among whom was Mr Logan, who remained with Mr Watt, counting altogether eleven persons. During the first and middle parts of these twenty-four hours the wind was from the east, blowing what seamen term 'fresh breezes'; but in the afternoon it shifted to E.N.E., accompanied with so heavy a swell of sea that the Smeaton was obliged to slip her moorings, and passed the tender, drifting before the wind, with only the foresail set. In passing, Mr Pool hailed that he must run for the Frith of Forth to prevent the vessel from 'riding under'.

On board of the tender the writer's chief concern was about the eleven men left upon the beacon. Directions were accordingly given that every thing about the vessel should be put in the best possible state, to present as little resistance to the wind as possible, that she might have the better chance of riding out the gale. Among these preparations the best bower cable was bent, so as to have a second anchor in readiness in case the mooring hawser should give way, that every means might be used for keeping the vessel within sight of the prisoners on the beacon, and thereby keep them in as good spirits as possible. From the same motive the boats were kept afloat, that they might be less in fear of the vessel leaving her station. At 7 p.m. one of the boats was unluckily filled with sea from a wave breaking into her, and it was with great difficulty that she could be baled out and got on board, with the loss of her oars, rudder, and loose thwarts. Such was the motion of the ship that in taking this boat on board her gunwale was stove in, and she otherwise received considerable damage. Night approached, but it was still found quite impossible to go near the rock. Consulting, therefore, the safety of the second boat, she also was hoisted on board of the tender.

At this time the cabins of the beacon were only partially covered, and had neither been provided with bedding nor a proper fire-place, while the stock of provisions was but slender. In these uncomfortable circumstances the people on the beacon were left for the night, nor was the situation of those on board of the tender much better. The rolling and pitching motion of the ship was excessive; and, excepting to those who had been accustomed to a residence in the floating-light, it seemed quite intolerable. Nothing was heard but the hissing of the winds and the creaking of the bulk-heads or partitions of the ship: the night was therefore spent in the most unpleasant reflections upon the condition of the people on the beacon, especially in the prospect of the tender being driven from her moorings. In these circumstances, daylight was eagerly looked for, and hailed with delight, as well by those afloat as by the artificers upon the rock.

At 6 a.m. the landing-master considered the weather to have somewhat moderated; and, from certain appearances of the sky, he was of opinion that a change for the better would soon take place. He accordingly proposed to attempt a landing at low-water, and either get the people off the rock, or at least ascertain what state they were in. At 9 a.m. he left the vessel with a boat well manned, carrying with him a supply of cooked provisions and a tea-kettle full of mulled port wine for the people on the beacon, who had not had any regular diet for about 30 hours, while they were exposed during that period, in a great measure, both to the winds and the sprays of the sea. The boat having succeeded in landing, she returned at 11 a.m. with the artificers, who had got off with considerable difficulty, and who were heartily welcomed by all on board.

Upon enquiry, it appeared that three of the stones last laid upon the building had been partially lifted from their beds by the force of the sea, and were now held only by the trenails, and that the cast-iron sheer-crane had been thrown down and completely broken. With regard to the beacon, the sea at high-water had lifted part of the mortar gallery or lowest floor, and washed away all the lime casks and other movable articles from it; but the principal parts of this fabric had sustained no damage. On pressing Messrs. Logan and Watt on the situation of things in the course of the night, Mr Logan emphatically said: 'That the beacon had an *ill-fared*[1] *twist* when the sea broke upon it at high water, but that they were not very apprehensive of danger'. On enquiring as to how they spent the night, it appeared that they had made shift to keep a small fire burning, and by means of some old sails defended themselves pretty well from the sea sprays.

It was particularly mentioned that by the exertions of James Glen, one of the joiners, a number of articles were saved from being washed off the mortar gallery. Glen was also very useful in keeping up the spirits of the forlorn party. In the early part of life he had undergone many curious adventures at sea, which he now recounted somewhat after the manner of the tales of the *Arabian Nights*. When one observed that the beacon was a most comfortless lodging, Glen would presently introduce some of his exploits and hardships, in comparison with which the state of things at the beacon bore an aspect of comfort and happiness. Looking to their slender stock of provisions, and their perilous and uncertain chance of speedy relief, he would launch out into an account of one of his expeditions in the North Sea, when the vessel, being much disabled in a storm, was driven before the wind with the loss of almost all their provisions; and the ship being much infested with rats, the crew hunted these vermin with great eagerness to help their scanty allowance. By such means Glen had the address to make his companions, in some measure, satisfied, or at least passive, with regard to their miserable prospects upon this half-tide rock in the middle of the ocean. This incident is noticed, more particularly, to shew the effects of such a happy turn of mind even under the most distressing and ill-fated circumstances.

[1] Ill-fared—ill formed; ugly.

## CHAPTER XVI

Bad weather continues for five days. First trip of the Patriot. The mortar-makers. The rope ladder fixed.

3RD JUNE. The wind was at N.W. today, so that the vessel rode with her stern towards the rock; and as it came to blow excessively hard, there was some danger, in the event of any thing giving way, that she might drift upon the rock. Accordingly Mr Taylor, who commanded the tender, came into the writer's cabin between 1 and 2 o'clock this morning, and after some consultation it was thought advisable to slip the hawser, and to stand with the ship towards the land. It then blew so fresh, that though the sails were double reefed when the vessel got under way, it was still found necessary to take in a third reef in the mainsail, and at 6 a.m. she got into the harbour of Arbroath.

In the work-yard the hewing or cutting of the several courses went on with great alacrity: the freestone masons were now at work as high as the twentieth and twenty-first courses, and the granite masons had completed the sixteenth course, which was now lying on the platform marked and ready for shipment.

9TH JUNE. The tender and Smeaton having remained in port till last evening, both vessels sailed for the rock, and reached their moorings at 5 o'clock a.m. The boats were immediately hoisted out, when the mill-wrights, joiners and smiths, ten in number, landed on the beacon with their foreman, and proceeded to the fitting up of the cabins. Notwithstanding the hazardous situation upon the beacon in which these artificers had lately been placed, Mr Watt, with his principal assistant James Glen, were not to be moved with trifles, and the work, as formerly, was continued by the joiners' squad of artificers during the whole day, trusting to the eventual prospect of their being taken off by the boats at night. The operations of the building-artificers continued only three hours today, and no more than four additional stones were laid.

The Patriot having now undergone a complete repair, she was loaded with stones for the first time, and the writer took a passage in her to the Bell Rock, when he had the pleasure of finding that she wrought or sailed extremely well.

12TH JUNE. The Smeaton having arrived from Arbroath with another cargo of stones, the rock had now a very busy appearance, the following vessels belonging to the service being at their respective moorings, viz. the lighthouse yacht: the Sir Joseph Banks Tender: the sloops Smeaton and Patriot, besides the Hedderwick and Fernie decked praam-boats; and at the distance of about two miles and a half, the floating-light was stationed.

17TH JUNE. At 8 a.m. the artificers and sailors, forty-five in number, landed on the rock, and after four hours' work seven stones were laid. As it blew fresh from the N.W. in the evening, it was found impracticable either to land the building-artificers, or to take the artificers off the beacon, and they were accordingly left there all night, but in circumstances very different from those of the 1st of this month. The house, being now in a more complete state, was provided with bedding, and they spent the night pretty well; though they complained of having been much disturbed at the time of high-water by the shaking and tremulous motion of their house, and by the plashing noise of the sea upon the mortar gallery. Here James Glen's versatile powers were again at work in cheering up those who seemed to be alarmed, and in securing every thing as far as possible. On this occasion he had only to recall to the recollections of some of them the former night which they had spent on the beacon, the wind and sea being then much higher, and their habitation in a far less comfortable state.

18TH JUNE. The weather having moderated today, the wind shifted to the westward. At a quarter past 9 a.m. the artificers landed from the tender, and had the pleasure to find their friends who had been left on the rock quite hearty, alleging that the beacon was the preferable quarters of the two. The builders laid 16 stones in four hours and a half, when the whole returned on board of the tender; and at 3 p.m. all hands, counting fifty-four, assembled upon deck to prayers.

19TH JUNE. The wind was at N.E. today, with gentle breezes, but accompanied by the heaviest swell of sea which had yet been observed at the Bell Rock. In the forenoon, the writer, accompanied by the landing-master, in a well manned boat, went off to observe the effect of the breach of the sea upon the building and apparatus. The work had now attained the height of about 8 feet, on which one of the cranes was erected, the top of which was about 30 feet above the low-water mark. In the course of this tide, the sea, at the meeting of the waves round the building, was observed to rise in the most beautiful conical jets of about 30 or 40 feet in diameter at the base, to the height of 10 or 15 feet above the crane.

20TH JUNE. At 11 a.m. the boats landed with much difficulty, in order to ascertain the state of the building and apparatus. On examination it was happily found that none of the stones was lost, and that those observed yesterday to have been lifted off their beds were the three which had not been trenailed, but which, being fortunately confined by two of the jumpers or boring-irons left in the trenail holes of the lower course, were thus held in their places.

24TH JUNE. At 2 p.m. the building-artificers again landed, and continued to work till a quarter past 8, when 40 of the stones formerly landed were now laid, making no fewer than 57 blocks which had been built today in the course of both tides.

When as many stones were built as comprised this day's work, the demand for mortar was proportionally increased, and the task of the mortar-makers on these occasions was both laborious and severe. This operation was chiefly performed by John Watt,—a strong active quarrier by profession,—who was a perfect character in his way, and extremely zealous in his department. While the operations of the mortar-makers continued, the forge upon their gallery was not generally in use; but, as the working-hours of the builders extended with the height of the building, the forge could not be so long wanted, and then a sad confusion often ensued upon the circumscribed floor of the mortar-gallery, as the operations of Watt and his assistants trenched greatly upon those of the smiths. The casks with the ingredients for the mortar, consisting of pozzolano, lime, and sand, were laid to hand by the sailors. These materials were lifted in spadefuls and thrown into the cast-iron mortar tubs, where they were beat with an iron-shod pestle to a consistency suitable to the respective purposes of the work. In these circumstances the boundary of the smiths was much circumscribed, and they were personally annoyed, especially in blowy weather, with the dust of the lime in its powdered state. The mortar-makers, on the other hand, were often not a little distressed with the heat of the fire and the sparks elicited on the anvil, and not inaptly complained that they were placed between the 'Devil and the deep sea'.

The work being now about 10 feet in height admitted of a rope-ladder being extended between the beacon and the building. By this 'Jacob's Ladder', as the seamen termed it, a communication was kept up with the beacon while the rock was considerably under water. In the same manner a rope furnished with a travelling-pulley was extended for the purpose of transporting the mortar-buckets, and other light articles, between the beacon and the building, which also proved a great convenience to the work. At this period the rope-ladder and tackle for the mortar had a descent from the beacon to the building; by and by they were on a level; and, towards the end of the season, when the solid part had attained its full height, the ascent was from the mortar-gallery to the building.

## *CHAPTER XVII*

## An accident to the crane. Michael Wishart injured. The building stands above high-water for the first time. The artificers lodge in the beacon-house.

30TH JUNE. The crane upon the building had to be raised today from the eighth to the ninth course, an operation which now required all the strength that could be mustered for working the guy-tackles; for as the top of the crane was at this time about 35 feet above the rock it became much more unmanageable. In order to give an additional purchase in tightening the tackle, one of the blocks of stone was suspended at the end of the movable beam of the crane, which, by adding greatly to the purchase or weight, tended to slacken the guys in the direction to which the beam with the stone was pointed, and thereby enabled the artificers more easily to brace them one after another. While the beam was thus loaded, and in the act of swinging round from one guy to another, a great strain was suddenly brought upon the opposite tackle, with the end of which the artificers had very improperly neglected to take a turn round some stationary object, which would have given them the complete command of the tackle. Owing to this simple omission, the crane, with the large stone at the end of the beam, fell upon the building with a terrible crash. The surrounding artificers immediately flew in every direction to get out of its way; but Michael Wishart, the principal builder, having unluckily stumbled upon one of the uncut trenails, fell upon his back. His body fortunately got between the movable beam and the upright shaft of the crane, and was thus saved; but his feet got entangled with the wheels of the crane, and were severely injured. Wishart, being a robust young man, endured his misfortune with wonderful firmness: he was laid upon one of the narrow framed beds of the beacon, and dispatched in a boat to the tender, where the writer was when this accident happened, not a little alarmed on missing the crane from the top of the building and at the same time seeing a boat rowing towards the vessel with great speed. When the boat came alongside with poor Wishart stretched upon a bed, covered with blankets, a moment of great anxiety followed, which was, however, much relieved when, on stepping into the boat, he was accosted by Wishart, though in a feeble voice, and with an aspect pale as death from excessive bleeding. Directions having been immediately given to the coxwain to apply to Mr Kennedy at the work-yard to procure the best surgical aid, the boat was sent off without delay to Arbroath. The writer then landed at the rock, when the crane was in a very short time got into its place and again put in a working state.

2ND JULY. The artificers commenced work at a quarter from 8 o'clock a.m., and continued for seven hours and a quarter, when seven blocks of stone were laid, with which the ninth course of the building was completed. The remainder of this long tide's work was occupied in boring trenail holes, driving trenails and wedges and in filling the perpendicular joints of the course with thin mortar, mixed up into that consistency which is technically termed grout. Having again landed in the evening, the same operation was continued from 8 till 11 o'clock p.m.; but the wind having shifted from south to E.N.E., it blew so fresh that the torches could not be kept burning, being now more exposed, and without the shelter which the foundation-pit formerly afforded. The work was, therefore, obliged to be dropped before the tide had overflowed the rock.

At midnight all hands left the rock in four boats, two of which belonged to the tender, one to the lighthouse yacht, and one to the Smeaton; and after much difficulty they reached their respective vessels. The yacht and Smeaton then slipped their moorings and proceeded for Arbroath, as they rode very hard, but the tender kept her position.

3RD JULY. The writer, having come to Arbroath with the yacht, had an opportunity of visiting Michael Wishart, the artificer who had met with so severe an accident at the rock on the 30th ult., and had the pleasure to find him in a state of recovery. Wishart expressed a hope that he might, at least, be ultimately capable of keeping the light at the Bell Rock, as it was not now likely that he would assist further in building the house.

8TH JULY. It was remarked today, with no small demonstration of joy, that the tide—being neap—did not, for the first time, overflow the building at high-water. Flags were accordingly hoisted on the beacon-house, and crane on the top of the building, which were repeated from the floating-light, lighthouse yacht, tender, Smeaton, Patriot, and the two praams. A salute of three guns was also fired from the yacht at high-water, when, all the artificers being collected on the top of the building, three cheers were given in testimony of this important circumstance. A glass of rum was then served out to all hands on the rock, and on board of the respective ships.

16TH JULY. The artificers landed at half-past 7, and laid 21 stones in the course of seven hours and a half; and having again landed in the evening at 7, they laid 11 stones in four hours, all of which had been landed on the rock today from the praams. Besides laying, boring, trenailing, wedging, and grouting these stones, several other operations were proceeded with on the rock at low-water, when some of the artificers were employed at the railways, and at high-water at the beacon-house. The seamen having prepared a quantity of tarpaulin, or cloth laid over with successive coats of hot tar, the joiners had just completed the covering of the roof with it. This sort of covering was lighter and more easily managed than sheet-lead in such a situation. As a further defence against the weather, the whole exterior of this temporary residence was painted with three coats of white-lead paint. Between the timber-framing of the habitable part of the beacon the interstices were to be stuffed with moss, as a light substance that would resist dampness and check sifting winds: the whole interior was then to be lined with green baize cloth, so that both without and within the cabins were to have a very comfortable appearance.

18TH JULY. The wind still continued to blow fresh from the N.E., but the artificers were enabled to land on the rock at a quarter from 11, where they remained two hours and three quarters, employed in shifting the crane on the building and making other preparations for laying the thirteenth course. Although the building-artificers generally remained on the rock throughout the day, and the mill-wrights, joiners, and smiths, while their number was considerable, remained also during the night, yet the tender had hitherto been considered as their night-quarters. But the wind having in the course of the day shifted to the N.W., and as the passage to the tender, in the boats, was likely to be attended with difficulty, the whole of the artificers, with Mr Logan, the foreman, preferred remaining all night on the beacon, which had of late become the solitary abode of George Forsyth, a jobbing-upholsterer, who had been employed in lining the beacon-house with cloth and in fitting up the bedding. Forsyth was a tall, thin, and rather loose-made man, who had an utter aversion at climbing upon the trap-ladders of the beacon, but especially at the process of boating, and the motion of the ship, which he said, 'was death itself'. He therefore pertinaciously insisted with the landing-master on being left upon the beacon, with a small black dog as his only companion. The writer, however, felt some delicacy in leaving a single individual upon the rock, who must have been so very helpless in case of accident. This fabric had, from the beginning, been rather intended by the writer to guard against accident from the loss or damage of a boat, and as a place for making mortar, a smith's shop, and a store for tools, during the working months, than as permanent quarters: nor was it at all meant to be possessed until the joiner-work was completely finished, and his own cabin, and that for the foremen, in readiness, when it was still to be left to the choice of the artificers to occupy the tender or the beacon. He, however, considered Forsyth's partiality and confidence in the latter as rather a fortunate occurrence.

The whole of the artificers, 23 in number, now removed, of their own accord from the tender to lodge in the beacon, together with Peter Fortune, a person singularly adapted for a residence of this kind, both from the urbanity of his manners and the versatility of his talents. Fortune, in his person, was of small stature, and rather corpulent. Besides being a good Scotch cook, he had acted both as groom and house-servant;

he had been a soldier, a suttler, a writer's clerk, and an apothecary, from which he possessed the art of writing and suggesting recipes, and had hence, also, perhaps acquired a turn for making collections in natural history. But in his practice in surgery on the Bell Rock, for which he received an annual fee of three guineas, he is supposed to have been rather partial to the use of the lancet. In short, Peter was the *factotum* of the beacon-house, where he ostensibly acted in the several capacities of cook, steward, surgeon, and barber, and kept a statement of the rations or expenditure of the provisions with the strictest integrity.

## *CHAPTER XVIII*

### Embargo upon shipping. The thirteenth course completed in haste. Special facilities given to Bell Rock shipping. Rough times at the beacon. Laying of twenty-fourth course completes the solid part of the building. Work ended for the season.

22ND JULY. In the present important state of the building, when it had just attained the height of 16 feet, and the upper courses, and especially the imperfect one, were in the wash of the heaviest seas, an express-boat arrived at the rock with a letter from Mr Kennedy of the work-yard, stating that in consequence of the intended Expedition to Walcheren, an embargo had been laid on shipping at all the ports of Great Britain; that both the Smeaton and Patriot were detained at Arbroath, and that, but for the proper view which Mr Ramsay, the port-officer, had taken of his orders, neither the express-boat, nor one which had been sent with provisions and necessaries for the floating-light would have been permitted to leave the harbour. The writer set off without delay for Arbroath, and on landing used every possible means with the official people; but their orders were deemed so peremptory that even boats were not permitted to sail from any port upon the coast.

At this critical period Mr Adam Duff, then Sheriff of Forfarshire, took an immediate interest in representing the circumstances of the case to the Board of Customs at Edinburgh. But such were the doubts entertained on the subject, that, on having previously received the appeal from the Collector at Montrose, the case had been submitted to the consideration of the Lords of the Treasury, whose decision was now waited for.

In this state of things the writer felt particularly desirous to get the thirteenth course finished, that the building might be in a more secure state in the event of bad weather. An opportunity was therefore embraced on the 25th, in sailing with provisions for the floating-light, to carry the necessary stones to the rock for this purpose, which were landed and built on the 26th and 27th. But so closely was the watch kept up, that a Custom-house officer was always placed on board of the Smeaton and Patriot while they were afloat, till the embargo was specially removed from the lighthouse vessels. The artificers at the Bell Rock had been reduced to fifteen, who were regularly supplied with provisions, along with the crew of the floating-light, mainly through the port-officer's liberal interpretation of his orders. After completing the thirteenth course, they were employed in erecting a kind of stool or prop of masonry on the western side of the building, for which the stones had fortunately been landed previous to the embargo. This prop consisted of large blocks of stone, and, when completed, it was 6 feet in height and 6 feet square at the top, so that the men in working the crane had a sufficient space for standing. By this means the foot of the lower crane was elevated 6 feet above the rock, which, added to the length of the working-beam, made a height of about 18 feet, and in the present state of the building the stones were thus raised to the level of the last built course. The crane on the top of the building, with which the stones were laid, was therefore now only employed to take them from the lower crane, instead of lifting them at once from the waggons on the railway.

The Lords of the Treasury had no sooner received the appeal from the Board of Customs at Edinburgh than an order was issued for all vessels and boats belonging to the service of the Commissioners of the Northern Lighthouses to be released and permitted to sail upon their respective voyages.

1ST AUGUST. Today no less than 78 blocks of stone were landed, of which 40 were built, which completed the fourteenth, and part of the fifteenth courses. Those daily at work upon the rock at this period amounted to 46. A cabin had been laid out for the writer on the beacon, but his apartment had been the last which was finished, and he had not yet taken possession of it; for though he generally spent the greater part of the day, at this time, upon the rock, yet he always slept on board of the tender.

11TH AUGUST. The wind was S.E. on the 11th, and there was so very heavy a swell of sea upon the rock that no boat could approach it. The sea broke with great violence both upon the building and the beacon. The former being 23 feet in height, the upper part of the crane erected on it having been lifted from course to course as the building advanced, was now about 36 feet above the rock. From observations made on the rise of the sea by this crane, the artificers were enabled to estimate its height to be about 50 feet above the rock, while the sprays fell with a most alarming noise upon their cabins. At low-water, in the evening, a signal was made from the beacon, at the earnest desire of some of the artificers, for the boats to come to the rock; and although this could not be effected without considerable hazard, it was, however, accomplished, when twelve of their number, being much afraid, applied to the foreman to be relieved, and went on board of the tender. But the remaining fourteen continued on the rock with Mr Peter Logan, the foreman builder. Although this rule of allowing an option to every man either to remain on the rock or return to the tender was strictly adhered to, yet, as it would have been extremely inconvenient to have had the men parcelled out in this manner, it became necessary to embrace the first opportunity of sending those who had left the beacon to the work-yard, with as little appearance of intention as possible, lest it should hurt their feelings, or prevent others from acting according to their wishes either in landing on the rock or remaining on the beacon.

13TH AUGUST. All hands were employed at low-water to-day in refitting the sheer-crane at the eastern landing-place, and in adjusting other things about the beacon and rock, which had been scattered and deranged during the late gale. The whole appurtenances of the mortar-gallery had been sent adrift; even the blacksmith's anvil was upset! and found lying at the foot of the beacon, while his bellows, and the greater part of the deals with which the floor was laid, were forced up and carried away, with all the lime and cement casks.

15TH AUGUST. The writer had this day taken possession of his cabin in the beacon-house. It was small, but commodious, and was found particularly convenient in coarse and blowing weather, instead of being obliged to make a passage to the tender in an open boat at all times both during the day and the night, which was often attended with much difficulty and danger.

20TH AUGUST. The weather being very favourable today, 53 stones were landed, and the builders were not a little gratified in having built the twenty-second course, consisting of 51 stones, being the first course which had been completed in one day. This, as a matter of course, produced three hearty cheers. At 12 noon, prayers were read for the first time on the Bell Rock: those present, counting thirty, were crowded into the upper apartment of the beacon, where the writer took a central position, while two of the artificers joining hands supported the Bible.

21ST AUGUST. The wind was from the S.W. this morning, blowing fresh, with rain. The praam-boats, however, landed thirty-two stones, which were also built. At 6 p.m. the Smeaton arrived from Arbroath, having on board the last cargo of the solid part of the building. She was, of course, decorated with all her colours; and, in compliment to the advanced state of the work, there was a display of flags from the floating-light and the other vessels on the station, and also from the beacon-house and the building itself.

25TH AUGUST. Today the remainder of the Smeaton's cargo was landed, and the artificers laid 45 stones, which completed the twenty-fourth course, reckoning above the first entire one, and the twenty-sixth above the rock. This finished the solid part of the building, and terminated the height of the outward casing of granite, which is 31 feet 6 inches above the rock or site of the foundation-stone, and about 17 feet above high-water of spring-tides. Being a particular crisis in the progress of the lighthouse, the landing and laying of the last stone for the season was observed with the usual ceremonies.

30TH AUGUST. The whole of the artificers left the rock at mid-day, when the tender made sail for Arbroath, which she reached about 6 p.m. The vessel being decorated with colours, and having fired a salute of three guns on approaching the harbour, the work-yard artificers, with a multitude of people, assembled at the harbour, when mutual cheering and congratulations took place between those afloat and those on the

The works at the rock in August 1809

quays. The tender had now, with little exception, been six months on the station at the Bell Rock, and during the last four months few of the squad of builders had been ashore. In particular, Mr Peter Logan, the foreman, and Mr Robert Selkirk, principal builder, had never once left the rock. The artificers having made good wages during their stay, like seamen upon a return-voyage were extremely happy, and spent the evening with much innocent mirth and jollity.

In reflecting upon the state of matters at the Bell Rock during the working months, when the writer was much with the artificers, nothing can equal the happy manner in which these excellent workmen spent their time. They always went from Arbroath to their arduous task cheering, and they generally returned in the same hearty state. While at the rock, between the tides, they amused themselves in reading, fishing, music, playing cards, draughts, etc., or in sporting with one another. In the work-yard at Arbroath the young men were, almost without exception, employed in the evening at school, in writing and arithmetic, and not a few were learning architectural drawing, for which they had every convenience and facility, and were, in a very obliging manner, assisted in their studies by Mr David Logan, Clerk of Works. It therefore affords the most pleasing reflections to look back upon the pursuits of about 60 individuals, who for years conducted themselves on all occasions in a sober and rational manner. Looking forward with confidence to the completion of the Bell Rock Lighthouse in the course of the next year, the writer, with much expectation, began to prepare every part of the establishment.

(Until November 1809 parties of workmen went to the rock during spring tides when the weather was favourable. They were employed in strengthening the beacon, completing the railways, and in making all safe for the winter.)

# OPERATIONS OF 1810

(From November 1809 to April 1810 the rock was occasionally visited by a party of five workmen in charge of Mr Francis Watt, the foreman mill-wright.

Meanwhile, all preparations were being made ashore in the hope of completing the lighthouse in the coming season. A balance-crane, specially designed by Stevenson for work at the top of the building, had been constructed; also a wooden bridge with which to connect the beacon and the lighthouse.)

## *CHAPTER XIX*

## The wooden bridge erected. The masons sail for the rock. Condition of the beacon-house after the winter.

18TH APRIL. Being fitted out for the rock with a sufficient stock of water and provisions, and having also on board the beams and apparatus for the wooden bridge, the tender sailed at 1 o'clock this morning with eleven masons, three joiners, and two black-smiths, together with Mr Francis Watt, foreman: in all seventeen artificers, who were to be employed during the ensuing spring-tides in erecting the bridge between the beacon and building. At 3 p.m. she was made fast to the new moorings, but the weather was then so boisterous that no landing could be made on the rock till the following morning at 6 o'clock, when they commenced the operations of the season by laying the deals of the mortar-gallery, or lowest floor of the beacon. The work now proceeded with so much alacrity and dispatch that by the 28th the fixing of the bridge was completed, and the tender returned with all hands to Arbroath.

7TH MAY. The artificers having been warned to take their quarters on board of the tender last night, the writer sailed this morning from Arbroath at half-past 2. At 12 noon the floating-light was hailed, when Captain Wilson, the landing-master, came on board to take his station for the season, and at 1 p.m. the tender was made fast to her moorings at the Bell Rock. The praam-boat was immediately hauled alongside, and the apparatus of the balance-crane laid upon her deck, when she was towed to her moorings, there being too much sea at this time for attempting to land upon the rock.

8TH MAY. The wind was at east today, and the sea still broke so heavily upon the rock that no landing could be made. At high-water the spray was observed to fly considerably above the building, perhaps not less than 20 feet, in all about 50 feet above the rock, while the seas were raging and breaking among the beams of the beacon with much violence.

9TH MAY. The same boisterous state of the weather still continued and the sea-swell was nothing abated today, so that no landing could yet be made upon the rock. The landing-master, however, went in a boat and examined the praam-boat at her moorings, where everything was found in good order. It is here worthy of remark that while the tender and floating-light rolled much, and occasionally shipped pretty heavy seas, the praam, with a cargo of about three tons on board, was perfectly dry upon deck, and, to use the seamen's expression, 'rode as easily as an old shoe'.

10TH MAY. The wind had shifted today to W.N.W., when the writer, with considerable difficulty, was enabled to land upon the rock for the first time this season, at 10 a.m. Upon examining the state of the building and apparatus in general, he had the satisfaction to find everything in good order. The mortar in all the joints was perfectly entire. The building, now 30 feet in height, was thickly coated with *fuci* to the height of about 15 feet, calculating from the rock: on the eastern side, indeed, the growth of sea-weed was observable to the full height of 30 feet, and even on the top or upper bed of the last laid course, especially towards the eastern side, it had germinated, so as to render walking upon it somewhat difficult. The smith's forge, which had been removed from the mortar-gallery to the top of the building in the month of September last to give more accommodation to the work of the joiners, had been left there for the season,—the bellows excepted, which were kept under cover in the beacon throughout the winter: and it is not a little remarkable that although the sea had risen to a considerable height, and fallen in great quantities upon the top of the building; yet such was the central position of the forge, that it remained quite entire. Even the spar of timber, and the small cords which had been stretched for steadying it and forming an awning of about 8 feet in diameter for sheltering the smith, were also still in their places. This was a proof that no very heavy seas had broken so high as the top of the solid, otherwise the forge and the apparatus for supporting the awning must have long since been swept away by the breach of the sea. The beacon-house was in a perfectly sound state, and apparently just as it had been left in the month of November.

Upon ascending to the apartments, it was found that the motion of the sea had thrown open the door of the cook-house: this was only shut with a simple latch, so that in case of shipwreck at the Bell Rock the mariner might find ready access to the shelter of this forlorn habitation, where a supply of provisions was kept; and being within two miles and a half of the floating-light, a signal could readily be observed, when a boat might be sent to his relief as soon as the weather permitted. An arrangement for this purpose formed one of the instructions on board of the floating-light, but happily no instance occurred for putting it in practice.

The writer next ascended to the floor which was occupied by the cabins of himself and his assistants, which were in tolerably good order, having only a damp and musty smell. The barrack for the artificers, over all, was next visited: it had now a very dreary and deserted appearance when its former thronged state was recollected. In some parts the water had come through the boarding, and had discoloured the lining of green cloth, but it was, nevertheless, in a good habitable condition. While the seamen were employed in landing a stock of provisions, a few of the artificers set to work, with great eagerness, to sweep and clean the several apartments. The exterior of the beacon was in the mean-time examined and found in perfect order. The painting, though it had a somewhat blanched appearance, adhered firmly both on the sides and roof, and only two or three panes of glass were broken in the cupola, which had either been blown out by the force of the wind, or perhaps broken by sea-fowl.

Having, on this occasion, continued upon the building and beacon a considerable time after the tide had begun to flow, the artificers were occupied in removing the forge from the top of the building, to which the gangway or wooden bridge gave great facility; and, although it stretched or had a span of 42 feet, its construction was extremely simple, while the road-way was perfectly firm and steady. In returning from this visit to the rock every one was pretty well soused in spray before reaching the tender at 2 o'clock p.m., where things awaited the landing-party in as comfortable a way as such a situation would admit.

## CHAPTER XX

### The balance-crane landed and erected. Rough weather delays the work. Prayers read on the lighthouse for the first time. The door lintel landed and laid.

11TH MAY. The wind was still easterly, accompanied with rather a heavy swell of sea for the operations in hand. A landing was, however, made this morning, when the artificers were immediately employed in scraping the sea-weed off the upper course of the building, in order to apply the moulds of the first course of the staircase, so that the joggle-holes might be marked off in the upper course of the solid, which, as formerly, had not been done to the finishing course of the season. This was also necessary previously to the writer's fixing the position of the entrance-door, which was regulated chiefly by the appearance of the growth of the sea-weed on the building, indicating the direction of the heaviest seas, on the opposite side of which the door was placed. The landing-master's crew succeeded in towing into the creek on the western side of the rock the praam-boat with the balance-crane, which had now been on board of the praam for five days. The several pieces of this machine having been conveyed along the railways upon the waggons to a position immediately under the bridge, were elevated to its level in the following manner. A chain-tackle was suspended over a pulley from the cross-beam connecting the tops of the king-posts of the bridge, which was worked by a winch-machine, with wheel, pinion and barrel, round which last the chain was wound. Immediately under the cross-beam a hatch was formed in the roadway of the bridge made to shut with folding boards like a double-door, through which stones

The bridge and the balance-crane, July 1810

and other articles were raised. In this manner, the several castings of the balance-crane were got up to the top of the solid of the building.

The several apartments of the beacon-house having been cleaned out and supplied with bedding, a sufficient stock of provisions was put into the store, when Peter Fortune, lighted his fire in the beacon for the first time this season. Sixteen artificers, at the same time, mounted to their barrack-room, and the foremen of the works also took possession of their cabin, all heartily rejoiced at getting rid of the trouble of boating and the sickly motion of the tender.

12TH MAY. The wind was at E.N.E., blowing so fresh, and accompanied with so much sea, that no stones could be landed today. The people on the rock, however, were busily employed in screwing together the balance-crane, cutting out the joggle-holes in the upper course, and preparing all things for commencing the building operations.

14TH MAY. The wind continued to blow so fresh that, on board of the tender, we were still without any communication with the people on the rock; where the sea was seen breaking over the top of the building in great sprays, and raging with much agitation among the beams of the beacon.

17TH MAY. The wind in the course of the day had shifted from north to west; the sea being also considerably less, a boat landed on the rock at 6 p.m., for the first time since the 11th, with the provisions and water brought off by the Patriot. The inhabitants of the beacon were all well, but tired above measure for want of employment, as the balance-crane and apparatus were all in readiness. In these circumstances they felt no less desirous of the return of good weather than those afloat, who were continually tossed with the agitation of the sea. The writer, in particular, felt himself almost as much fatigued and worn out as he had been at any period since the commencement of the work. The very backward state of the weather at so advanced a period of the season unavoidably created some alarm, lest he should be overtaken with bad weather at a late period of the season, with the building operations in an unfinished state. This being also his first off-set for the season, every bone of his body felt sore with preserving a sitting posture, while he endeavoured to pass away the time in reading; as for writing it was wholly impracticable. He had several times entertained thoughts of leaving the station for a few days, and going into Arbroath with the tender till the weather should improve; but, as the artificers had been landed on the rock, he was averse to this at the commencement of the season, knowing also that he would be equally uneasy in every situation till the first cargo was landed; and he therefore resolved to continue at his post until this should be effected.

18TH MAY. The wind being now N.W., the sea was considerably run down, and this morning at 5 o'clock the landing-master's crew, thirteen in number, left the tender, and in the course of the day twenty-three blocks of stone, three casks of pozzolano, three of sand, three of lime, and one of Roman cement, together with three bundles of trenails and three of wedges, were all landed on the rock and raised to the top of the building by means of the tackle suspended from the cross-beam on the middle of the bridge. The stones were then moved along the bridge on the waggon to the building, within reach of the balance-crane, with which they were laid in their respective places on the building. When the first stone was to be suspended by the balance-crane, the bell on the beacon was rung, and all the artificers and seamen were collected on the building. Three hearty cheers were given while the stone was lowered into its place, and the steward served round a glass of rum, when success was drunk to the further progress of the building.

Having thus had the satisfaction of finding that the bridge and its apparatus answered every purpose for raising the materials; that the balance-crane was no less suitable for building the stones, and the artificers being now comfortably lodged in the beacon-house, there hardly remained a doubt that the Bell Rock Lighthouse would be completed in the course of the current year. It often happens, however, that accidents occur on the first trial of machinery: and, accordingly, in shifting the wheel and pinion work of the winch-machine upon the bridge in order to raise a pretty heavy stone, the bolt of the bush gave way, just as the stone had attained its full height and was about to be lowered on the bridge-waggon. The fall of the stone, though only from a height of 8 or 9 inches, communicated a sudden shock throughout the beacon-house, and produced an alarm among the workmen for the moment. Had this accident occurred before the waggon was wheeled under the stone, in all probability it would have killed some of those who were at work below upon the rock; besides breaking the stone and the railway, which must have stopped the work for a considerable time until another stone could have been prepared and sent from the work-yard at Arbroath.

20TH MAY. The artificers had completed the laying of the twenty-seventh course or first course of the staircase this morning, and in the evening they finished the boring, trenailing, wedging, and grouting it with mortar. At 12 o'clock noon the beacon-house bell was rung, and all hands were collected on the top of the building, where prayers were read for the first time on the lighthouse, which had, upon the whole, a very impressive effect.

25TH MAY. The landing operations proceeded briskly, so that the building was today ready for the door-lintel.

The door-lintel being of large dimensions, equal to about a ton and a half in weight, and considerably heavier than any of the stones of this course, in raising it with the balance-crane sufficient attention had not been paid to increase the balance-weight proportionally, and an unequal strain being then brought upon the opposite arms of the crane, the upright shaft yielded and broke at one of the joints. Fortunately no person was hurt, though a stop was put to the work for the present. This unlucky accident happened about 4 in the afternoon, when the Patriot, then at her moorings discharging a cargo of stones, was immediately dispatched to Arbroath with the broken shaft, where she arrived about 2 o'clock on Sunday morning. The writer was at this early hour rather alarmed by Captain Macdonald knocking at his bed-room door, and calling out in a hollow tone 'that the balance-crane had given way'. An express was immediately sent for Mr James Dove, who, only two days prior to the accident, had left the Bell Rock, and was in the neighbourhood of Arbroath, and, when the messenger reached him, was preparing to go with his friends to the church of his native parish.

This accident, though speedily repaired, produced a delay of no less than three days to the building operations, which, together with the time occupied in making provision for a new method of inserting the door-hinges into the building, made this part of the masonry, upon the whole, appear extremely tedious. Having got the door-lintel laid, the writer was not a little gratified on being welcomed, with acclamation, in at the door of the Bell Rock Lighthouse. Limited as the height of the building still was, the formation of the door stamped a new character upon it, and the lintel gave it an additional appearance of strength.

## *CHAPTER XXI*

## Progress ashore. The store-room floor completed. The first letter dated from the lighthouse. Heavy seas break on the building. Wet weather.

While the work thus proceeded at the Bell Rock, it was making also good progress at Arbroath, as the whole of the courses, excepting three, were now ready for shipping to the rock. Advice was also received from Edinburgh that the light-room reflecting apparatus and revolving machinery were getting regularly forward, so that every prospect was afforded of the work being brought to a conclusion in the course of the season.

As the lighthouse advanced in height, the cubical contents of the stones were less, but they had to be raised to a greater height; and the walls being thinner were less commodious for the necessary machinery and the artificers employed, which considerably retarded the work. Inconvenience was also occasionally experienced from the men dropping their coats, hats, mallets and other tools, at high-water, which were carried away by the tide; and the danger to the people themselves was now greatly increased. Had any of them fallen from the beacon or building at high-water while the landing-master's crew were generally engaged with the craft at a distance, it must have rendered the accident doubly painful to those on the rock, who at this time had no boat, and consequently no means of rendering immediate and prompt assistance. In such cases, it would have been too late to have got a boat by signal from the tender. A small boat, which could be lowered at pleasure, was therefore suspended by a pair of davits projected from the cook-house, the keel being about 30 feet from the rock. This boat, with its tackle, was put under the charge of James Glen, of whose exertions on the beacon mention has already been made, and who having in early life been a seaman, was also very expert in the management of a boat. A life-buoy was likewise suspended from the bridge, to which a coil of line 200 fathoms in length was attached, which could be let out to a person falling into the water, or to the people in the boat, should they not be able to work her with the oars.

7TH JUNE. The Bell Rock works had now a very busy appearance, as the lighthouse was daily getting more into form. Besides the artificers and their cook, the writer and his servant were also lodged on the beacon, counting in all twenty-nine; and at low-water the landing-master's crew, consisting of from twelve to fifteen seamen, were employed in transporting the building materials, working the landing apparatus on the rock, and dragging the stone-waggons along the railways.

14TH JUNE. Today 27 stones and 11 joggle pieces were landed, part of which consisted of the forty-seventh course, forming the store-room floor. The builders were at work this morning by 4 o'clock, in the hopes of being able to accomplish the laying of the 18 stones of this course. But at 8 o'clock in the evening they had still two to lay, and as the stones of this course were very unwieldy, being 6 feet in length, they required much precaution and care both in lifting and laying them. It was, however, only on the writer's suggestion to Mr Logan that the artificers were induced to leave off, as they had intended to complete this floor before going to bed. The two remaining stones were, however, laid in their places without mortar, when the bell on the beacon was rung, and all hands being collected on the top of the building, three hearty cheers were given on covering the first apartment. The steward then served out a dram to each, when the whole retired to their barrack much fatigued, but with the anticipation of the most perfect repose even in the 'hurricane-house' amidst the dashing seas on the Bell Rock.

While the workmen were at breakfast and dinner it was the writer's usual practice to spend his time on the walls of the building, which, notwithstanding the narrowness of the track, nevertheless formed his principal walk when the rock was under water. But this afternoon he had his writing-desk set upon the store-room floor, when he wrote to Mrs Stevenson certainly the first letter dated from the Bell Rock *Lighthouse*, giving a detail of the fortunate progress of the work, with an assurance that the lighthouse would soon be completed at the rate at which it now proceeded. The Patriot having sailed for Arbroath in the evening, he felt no small degree of pleasure in dispatching this communication to his family.

15TH JUNE. It was a general remark at the Bell Rock, as before noticed, that fish were never plenty in its neighbourhood excepting in good weather. Indeed, the seamen used to speculate about the state of the weather from their success in fishing. When the fish disappeared at the rock, it was considered a sure indication that a gale was not far off, as the fish seemed to seek shelter in deeper water from the roughness of the sea during these changes of the weather. At this time the rock, at high-water, was completely covered with podlies, or the fry of the coalfish, about six or eight inches in length. The artificers sometimes occupied half an hour after breakfast and dinner in catching these little fishes, but were more frequently supplied from the boats of the tender.

17TH JUNE. The wind blew very hard in the course of last night from N.E., and to-day the sea ran so high that no boat could approach the rock. During the dinner-hour, when the writer was going to the top of the building as usual, but just as he entered the door and was about to ascend the ladder, a great noise was heard overhead, and in an instant he was soused in water from a sea which had most unexpectedly come over the walls, though now about 58 feet in height. On making his retreat he found himself completely whitened by the lime which had mixed with the water while dashing down through the different floors; and, as nearly as he could guess, a quantity equal to about a hogshead had come over the walls, and now streamed out at the door. The incident just noticed did not create more surprise in the mind of the writer than the sublime appearance of the waves as they rolled majestically over the rock. This scene he greatly enjoyed while sitting at his cabin window: each wave approached the beacon like a vast scroll unfolding; and in passing discharged a quantity of air, which he not only distinctly felt, but was even sufficient to lift the leaves of a book which lay before him.

19TH JUNE. The 19th was a very unpleasant and disagreeable day both for the seamen and artificers, as it rained throughout with little intermission from 4 a.m. till 11 p.m., accompanied with thunder and lightning, during which period the work nevertheless continued unremittingly; and the builders laid the fifty-first and fifty-second courses. This state of weather was no less severe upon the mortar-makers, who required to temper or prepare the mortar of a thicker or thinner consistency, in some measure, according to the state of the weather. On occasions like the present, however, there was often a difference of opinion between the builders and the mortar-makers. John Watt, who had the principal charge of the mortar, was a most active worker, but being somewhat of an irascible temper, the builders occasionally amused themselves at his expense: for while he was eagerly at work with his large iron-shod pestle in the mortar-tub, they often sent down contradictory orders, some crying,

'Make it a little stiffer, or thicker, John', while others called out to make it 'thinner', to which he generally returned very speedy and sharp replies; so that these conversations at times were rather amusing.

During wet weather the situation of the artificers on the top of the building was extremely disagreeable; for although their work did not require great exertion, yet, as each man had his particular part to perform, either in working the crane or in laying the stones, it required the closest application and attention, not only on the part of Mr Peter Logan, the foreman, who was constantly on the walls, but also of the chief workmen. Robert Selkirk, the principal builder, for example, had every stone to lay in its place. David Cumming, a mason, had the charge of working the tackle of the balance-weight, and James Scott, also a mason, took charge of the purchase with which the stones were laid; while the pointing the joints of the walls with cement was entrusted to William Reid and William Kennedy, who stood upon a scaffold suspended over the walls in rather a frightful manner. The least act of carelessness or inattention on the part of any of these men might have been fatal, not only to themselves but also to the surrounding workmen, especially if any accident had happened to the crane itself, while the material damage or loss of a single stone would have put an entire stop to the operations, until another could have been brought from Arbroath.

## *CHAPTER XXII*

# Discontent among the seamen. Two men dismissed the service. Heavy weather damages the beacon. The writer's cabin. The last cargo of stones loaded at Arbroath.

22ND JUNE. The duty of the landing-master's crew had, upon the whole, been easy of late; for though the work was occasionally irregular, yet, the stones being lighter, they were more speedily lifted from the hold of the stone-vessel to the deck of the praam-boat, and again to the waggons on the railway, after which they came properly under the charge of the foreman-builder. It is, however, a strange though not an uncommon feature in the human character that when people have least to complain of, they are most apt to become dissatisfied, as was now the case with the seamen employed in the Bell Rock service about their rations of beer. This being represented to the writer, he sent for Captain Wilson, the landing-master, and Mr Taylor, commander of the tender, with whom he talked over the subject. They stated that they considered the daily allowance of the seamen in every respect ample, and that, the work being now much lighter than formerly, they had no just ground for complaint; Mr Taylor adding that if those who now complained 'were even to be fed upon soft bread and turkeys, they would not think themselves right'.

(The landing-master's crew sent a written complaint to the lighthouse about their allowance of beer. Stevenson went to the tender to deal with the matter.)

At 7 o'clock the writer left the Bell Rock, after a residence of four successive weeks in the beacon-house. The first thing which occupied his attention on board of the tender was to look

General view of the Bell Rock works at low tide, July 1810

round upon the lighthouse, which he saw, with some degree of emotion and surprise, now vying in height with the beacon-house; for although he had often viewed it from the extremity of the western railway on the rock, yet the scene, upon the whole, seemed far more interesting from the tender's moorings, at the distance of about half a mile.

(Stevenson pointed out to the men that their allowance of beer was in accordance with their agreement. Two of the most discontented men were sent ashore and dismissed the service, whereupon the rest 'expressed themselves as satisfied'.)

28TH JUNE. The sixty-third and sixty-fourth courses were laid today, consisting of 16 stones each. Last night the wind had shifted to north-east, and, blowing fresh, was accompanied with a heavy surf upon the rock. Towards high-water it had a very grand and wonderful appearance. Waves of considerable magnitude rose as high as the solid or level of the entrance-door, which, being open to the south-west, was fortunately to the leeward; but on the windward side the sprays flew like lightning up the sloping sides of the building; and although the walls were now elevated 64 feet above the rock, and about 52 feet from high-water mark, yet the artificers were nevertheless wetted, and occasionally interrupted, in their operations on the top of the walls. These appearances were in a great measure new at the Bell Rock, there having till of late been no building to conduct the seas, or object to compare them with. The effects of these seas, as they raged among the beams, and dashed upon the higher parts of the beacon, produced a temporary tremulous motion throughout the whole fabric which to a stranger must have been frightful.

1ST JULY. The writer had now been at the Bell Rock since the latter end of May, or about six weeks, during four of which he had been a constant inhabitant of the beacon without having been once off the rock. After witnessing the laying of the sixty-seventh course, or second course of the bed-room apartment, he left the rock with the tender and went ashore, as some arrangements were to be made for the future conduct of the works at Arbroath, which were soon to be brought to a close. In leaving the rock, the writer kept his eyes fixed upon the light-house, which had recently got into the form of a house, having several tiers or storeys of windows. Nor was he unmindful of his habitation in the beacon, now far overtopped by the masonry; where he had spent several weeks in a kind of active retirement, making practical experiment of the fewness of the positive wants of man. His cabin measured not more than 4 feet 3 inches in breadth on the floor; and though, from the oblique direction of the beams of the beacon, it widened towards the top, yet it did not admit of the full extension of his arms when he stood on the floor; while its length was little more than sufficient for suspending a cot-bed during the night, calculated for being triced up to the roof through the day, which left free room for the admission of occasional visitants. His folding-table was attached with hinges immediately under the small window of the apartment, and his books, barometer, thermometer, portmanteau, and two or three camp-stools, formed the bulk of his movables. His diet being plain, the paraphernalia of the table were proportionally simple: though every thing had the appearance of comfort, and even of neatness, the walls being covered with green cloth formed into panels with red tape, and his bed festooned with curtains of yellow cotton-stuff. If, in speculating upon the abstract wants of man in such a state of exclusion, one were reduced to a single book, the Sacred Volume—whether considered for the striking diversity of its story, the morality of its doctrine, or the important truth of its Gospel—would have proved by far the greatest treasure.

4TH JULY. From the force of the wind, being now the period of spring-tides, a very heavy swell was experienced at the rock. At 2 o'clock in the morning the people on the beacon were in state of great alarm about their safety, as the sea had broke up part of the floor of the mortar-gallery, which was thus cleared of the lime-casks and other buoyant articles; and the alarm-bell being rung, all hands were called to render what assistance was in their power for the safety of themselves and the materials. At this time, some would willingly have left the beacon and gone into the building: the sea, however, ran so high that there was no passage along the bridge of communication; and when the interior of the lighthouse came to be examined in the morning, it appeared that great quantities of water had come over the walls, now 80 feet in height, and had run down through the several apartments, and out at the entrance-door. From this state of things the work was stopped for two days, in the course of which the joiners got the mortar-gallery refitted, and the landing-master's crew supplied it with a fresh stock of materials for making mortar. Notwithstanding this state of the sea upon the rock, the tender and Patriot still kept at their moorings. Such, indeed, was the practice of the seamen in this kind of life, that unless the wind blew from the N.W., or in such a direction as made the vessels ride with their sterns towards the rock, they never thought of moving from their moorings unless the vessels were deeply loaded.

9TH JULY. At Arbroath, the Patriot had now loaded the last cargo of building materials from that port. From the interest which the inhabitants of Arbroath took in all that concerned the Bell Rock Lighthouse, it soon became generally known that the last cargo from the work-yard was loading. Upon this occasion, the ships in the harbour hoisted their colours in compliment to the approaching termination of the works; and at 7 p.m. a great concourse of people collected on the quays, who united in giving three hearty cheers as the Patriot sailed from the harbour.

12TH JULY. The building-artificers laid the seventy-fourth course today, being the floor of the library or strangers' room, which, like the others, consisted altogether of 18 stones; but of the floor courses only sixteen stones were laid in the first instance, the centre and the stone connected with the man-hole being left for the convenience of moving the machinery as the building advanced in height. The seamen landed 25 blocks of stone and the remaining 2 dove-tailed joggles, which discharged the Patriot; and at 2 p.m. she sailed for Leith to load a cargo of the upper courses of the lighthouse, which had been worked at Edinburgh.

(The Smeaton had also proceeded to Leith for materials.)

## *CHAPTER XXIII*

# The last principal stone loaded at Leith. The completion of the masonry. The condition of the artificers. They leave the rock.

21ST JULY. The Smeaton now lay in Leith loaded; but the wind and weather being unfavourable for her getting down the Frith, she did not sail till this afternoon. It may here be proper to notice that the loading of the centre of the light-room floor, or last principal stone of the building, did not fail to excite an interest among those connected with the work. When the stone was laid upon the cart to be conveyed to Leith, the seamen fixed an ensign-staff and flag into the circular hole in the centre of the stone, and decorated their own hats, and that of James Craw, the Bell Rock carter, with ribbons; even his faithful and trusty horse Bassey was ornamented with bows and streamers of various colours. The masons also provided themselves with new aprons; and in this manner the cart was attended in its progress to the ship. When the cart came opposite the Trinity House of Leith, the officer of that Corporation made his appearance dressed in his uniform, with his staff of office. When it reached the harbour, the shipping in the different tiers where the Smeaton lay hoisted their colours, manifesting by these trifling ceremonies the interest with which the progress of this work was regarded by the public, as ultimately tending to afford safety and protection to the mariner.

26TH JULY. The artificers had finished the laying of the balcony course, excepting the centre stone of the light-room floor, which, like the centres of the other floors, could not be laid in its place till after the removal of the foot and shaft of the balance-crane. This stone was accordingly left on board of the Smeaton, to be landed with the last cargo. The eighty-sixth course, consisting of 8 stones, being the first of the parapet wall of the light-room, was landed and built. During the dinner hour, when the men were off work, the writer generally took some exercise by walking round the walls when the rock was under water. But today his boundary was greatly enlarged, for, instead of the narrow wall as a path, he felt no small degree of pleasure in walking round the balcony and passing out and in at the space allotted for the light-room door. In the labours of this day both the artificers and seamen felt their work to be extremely easy compared with what it had been for some days past.

29TH JULY. Captain Wilson and his crew had made preparations for landing the last stone, and, as may well be supposed, this was a day of great interest at the Bell Rock. 'That it might lose none of its honours', as he expressed himself, the Hedderwick praam-boat, with which the first stone of the building had been landed, was appointed also to carry the last. At 7 o'clock this evening the seamen hoisted three flags upon the Hedderwick, when the colours of the Dickie praam-boat, tender, Smeaton, floating-light, beacon-house, and lighthouse, were also displayed, and, the weather being remarkably fine, the whole presented a very gay appearance, and the effect was very pleasing. The praam which carried the stone was towed by the seamen in gallant style to the rock, and, on its arrival, cheers were given as a finale to the landing department.

30TH JULY. The ninetieth or last course of the building having been laid today, which brought the masonry to the height of 102 feet 6 inches, the lintel of the light-room door, being the finishing-stone of the exterior walls, was laid with due formality by the writer, who, at the same time, pronounced the following benediction: 'May the Great Architect of the Universe, under whose blessing this perilous work has prospered, preserve it as a guide to the Mariner'.

3RD AUGUST. At 3 p.m., the necessary preparations having been made, the artificers commenced the completing of the floors of the several apartments, and at 7 o'clock the centre-stone of the light-room floor was laid, which may be held as finishing the masonry of this important national edifice. After going through the usual ceremonies observed by the Brotherhood on occasions of this kind, the writer, addressing himself to the artificers and seamen who were present, briefly alluded to the utility of the undertaking as a monument of the wealth of British Commerce, erected through the spirited measures of the Commissioners of the Northern Lighthouses by means of the able assistance of those who now surrounded him. He then took an opportunity of stating that toward those connected with this arduous work he would ever retain the most heartfelt regard in all their interests.

4TH AUGUST. When the bell was rung as usual on the beacon this morning, every one seemed as if he were at a loss what to make of himself. There was, however, still much to do to the lighthouse, which is only yet to be considered in the state of a house with its outward wall built; but, before being useful or habitable, it must be roofed over, internally finished, and provided with the necessary furniture and utensils. The Sir Joseph Banks Tender had by this time been afloat, with little intermission, for six months, during the greater part of which the artificers had been almost constantly off at the rock, and were now much in want of necessaries of almost every description. Not a few had lost different articles of their clothing, which had dropped into the sea from the beacon and building; some wanted jackets, others, from want of hats, wore night-caps; each was, in fact, more or less curtailed in his wardrobe, and it must be confessed that at best the party were but in a very tattered condition. This morning was occupied in removing the artificers and their bedding on board of the tender; and although their personal luggage was easily shifted, the boats had, nevertheless, many articles to remove from the beacon-house, and were consequently employed in this service till 11 a.m. All hands being collected and just ready to embark, as the water had nearly overflowed the rock, the writer, in taking leave, after alluding to the harmony which had ever marked the conduct of those employed on the Bell Rock, took occasion to compliment the great zeal, attention and abilities of Mr Peter Logan and Mr Francis Watt, foremen, Captain James Wilson, landing-master, and Captain David Taylor, commander of the tender, who, in their several departments, had so faithfully discharged the duties assigned to them, often under circumstances the most difficult and trying. The health of these gentlemen was drunk with much warmth of feeling by the artificers and seamen, who severally expressed the satisfaction they had experienced in acting under them; after which the whole party left the rock.

5TH AUGUST. The writer has formerly noticed the uniformly decent and orderly deportment of the artificers who were employed at the Bell Rock Lighthouse and today, it is believed, they very generally attended church, no doubt with grateful hearts for the many narrow escapes from personal danger which all of them had more or less experienced during their residence at the Rock.

(On 14th August, 1810, the Smeaton was loaded at Leith with the iron window-frames for the light-room and the stone steps for the building.)

14TH AUGUST. With these she sailed to-day at 1 p.m., having on board 16 artificers, with Mr Peter Logan, together with a supply of provisions and necessaries; who left the harbour pleased and happy to find themselves once more afloat in the Bell Rock service. At 7 o'clock the tender was made fast to her moorings, when the artificers landed on the rock and took possession of their old quarters in the beacon-house, with feelings very different from those of 1807, when the works commenced.

## *CHAPTER XXIV*

# The tender goes adrift in a gale. Condition of the party left at the rock. More damage to the beacon. A fatal accident.

15TH AUGUST. The wind in the course of this day increased to a strong gale, accompanied with a sea which broke with great violence upon the rock. At 12 noon the tender rode very heavily at her moorings, when her chain broke at about 10 fathoms from the ship's bows. The kedge-anchor was immediately let go, but while this was in operation the hawser of the kedge was chafed through on the rocky bottom, and parted, when the vessel was again adrift. Most fortunately, however, she cast off with her head from the rock, and narrowly cleared it; when she sailed up the Frith of Forth to wait the return of better weather. The artificers were thus left upon the rock with so heavy a sea running that it was ascertained to have risen to the height of 80 feet on the building. Under such perilous circumstances it would be difficult to describe the feelings of those who, at this time, were cooped up in the beacon in so forlorn a situation, with the sea not only raging under them, but occasionally falling from a great height upon the roof of their temporary lodging, without even the attending vessel in view to afford the least gleam of hope in the event of any accident. It is true that they had now the masonry of the lighthouse to resort to, which, no doubt, lessened the actual danger of their situation. But the building was still without a roof, and the dead-lights, or storm shutters, not being yet fitted, the windows of the lower storey were stove in and broken, and at high-water the sea ran in considerable quantities out at the entrance-door. In the course of this afternoon, the spring-tides being now at the highest, the bridge or gangway was also for a time rendered completely impassable from the quantity of sea that constantly washed over it.

16TH AUGUST. The gale continued with unabated violence today, and the sprays rose to a still greater height, having been carried over the masonry of the building, or about 90 feet above the level of the sea. At 4 o'clock this morning, the sea was breaking into the cook's berth, when he rang the alarm-bell, and all hands turned out to attend to their personal safety. The floor of the smith's or mortar-gallery was now completely burst up by the force of the sea, and the cast-iron mortar-tubs, the iron hearth of the forge, the smith's bellows, and even his anvil, were thrown down upon the rock. The boarding of the cook-house, or storey above the smith's gallery, was also partly carried away, and the brick and plaster-work of the fire-place shaken and loosened. In this state of the weather, Captain Wilson and the crew of the floating-light were much alarmed for the safety of the artificers upon the rock, especially when they observed with a telescope that the floor of the smith's gallery had been carried away. It was quite impossible, however, to do anything for their relief until the gale should take off.

18TH AUGUST. The wind shifted to the westward today, and the tender got into Arbroath. In the mean time Captain Wilson visited the Bell Rock with a well manned boat from the floating-light, when he had the happiness to find Mr Peter Logan and his people in perfect health, though, in the course of the gale, they had at times been considerably alarmed while the sea was making inroads upon their habitation. In searching about the rock in quest of some of the articles which had been washed from the smith's gallery, it is not a little remarkable that so ponderous an article as the anvil, weighing 170 lbs., should have been found in a hole at the distance of 60 feet from the beacon, and that the iron pan or hearth of the forge, weighing about 100 lbs., was found at the distance of 200 feet from it. Near to this lay one of the cast-iron mortar-tubs; but the smith's bellows, and many other articles missing, were never found.

27TH AUGUST. The sash frames of the light-room, 8 in number, having been safely got up to the top of the building, were ranged on the balcony in the order in which they were numbered for their places on the top of the parapet-wall; and the balance-crane, that useful machine, having now lifted all the heavier articles, was unscrewed and lowered, to use the landing-master's phrase, 'in mournful silence'.

2ND SEPTEMBER. The steps of the stair being landed and all the weightier articles of the light-room got up to the balcony, the wooden bridge was now to be removed, as it had a very powerful effect upon the beacon when a heavy sea struck it; and could not possibly have withstood the storms of a winter. Every thing having been cleared from the bridge, and nothing left but the two principal beams with their horizontal braces, James Glen, at high-water, proceeded with a saw to cut through the beams at the end next the beacon, which likewise disengaged their opposite extremity, inserted a few inches into the building. The frame was then gently lowered into the water, and floated off to the Smeaton, to be towed to Arbroath. After the removal of the bridge, the aspect of things at the rock was much altered. The beacon-house and building had both a naked look to those accustomed to their former appearance; a curious optical deception was also remarked, by which the lighthouse seemed to incline from the perpendicular towards the beacon. The horizontal rope-ladder before noticed was again stretched to preserve the communication; and the artificers were once more obliged to practise the awkward and straddling manner of their passage between them during 1809.

At 12 noon the bell rang for prayers, after which the artificers went to dinner, when the writer passed along the rope-ladder to the lighthouse, and went through the several apartments, which were now cleared of lumber. In the afternoon all hands were summoned to the interior of the house, when he had the satisfaction of laying the upper step of the stair, or last stone of the building. This ceremony concluded with three cheers, the sound of which had a very loud and strange effect within the walls of the lighthouse.

14TH OCTOBER. The writer landed at the Bell Rock on Sunday the 14th of October, and had the pleasure to find, from the very favourable state of the weather, that the artificers had been enabled to make great progress with the fitting up of the light-room.

16TH OCTOBER. The light-room work had proceeded as usual today under the direction of Mr Dove. The artificers were at work till 7 o'clock p.m., and it being then dark, Mr Dove gave orders to drop work in the light-room; and all hands proceeded from thence to the beacon-house, when Charles Henderson, smith, and Henry Dickson, brazier, left the work together. Being both young men, who had been for several weeks upon the rock, they had become familiar, and even playful, on the most difficult parts about the beacon and building. This evening they were trying to out-run each other in descending from the light-room, when Henderson led the way; but they were in conversation with each other till they came to the rope-ladder extended between the entrance-door of the lighthouse and the beacon. Dickson, on reaching the cook-room, was surprised at not seeing his companion, and inquired hastily for Henderson. Upon which the cook replied, 'Was he before you upon the rope-ladder?' Dickson answered 'Yes; and I thought I heard something fall'. Upon this the alarm was given, and links were immediately lighted, with which the artificers descended on the legs of the beacon as near the surface of the water as possible, it being then about full tide, and the sea breaking to a considerable height upon the building, with the wind at S.S.E. But after watching till low-water, and searching in every direction upon the rock, it appeared that poor Henderson must have unfortunately fallen through the rope-ladder, and been washed into the deep water.

The deceased had passed along this rope-ladder many hundred times, both by day and night, and the operations in which he was employed being nearly finished, he was about to leave the rock when this melancholy catastrophe took place. The unfortunate loss of Henderson cast a deep gloom upon the minds of all who were at the rock, and it required some management on the part of those who had charge to induce the people to remain patiently at their work. As the weather now became more boisterous, and the nights long, they found their habitation extremely cheerless, while the winds were howling about their ears, and the waves lashing with fury against the beams of their isolated habitation.

## *CHAPTER XXV*

## The light-room completed and glazed. A difficult landing. The final inspection of lighthouse and beacon. Light-keepers left at the rock. The apparatus of the light fitted up.

25TH OCTOBER. The glazing of the sash-frames of the light-room having been completed on Wednesday the 24th, the boats

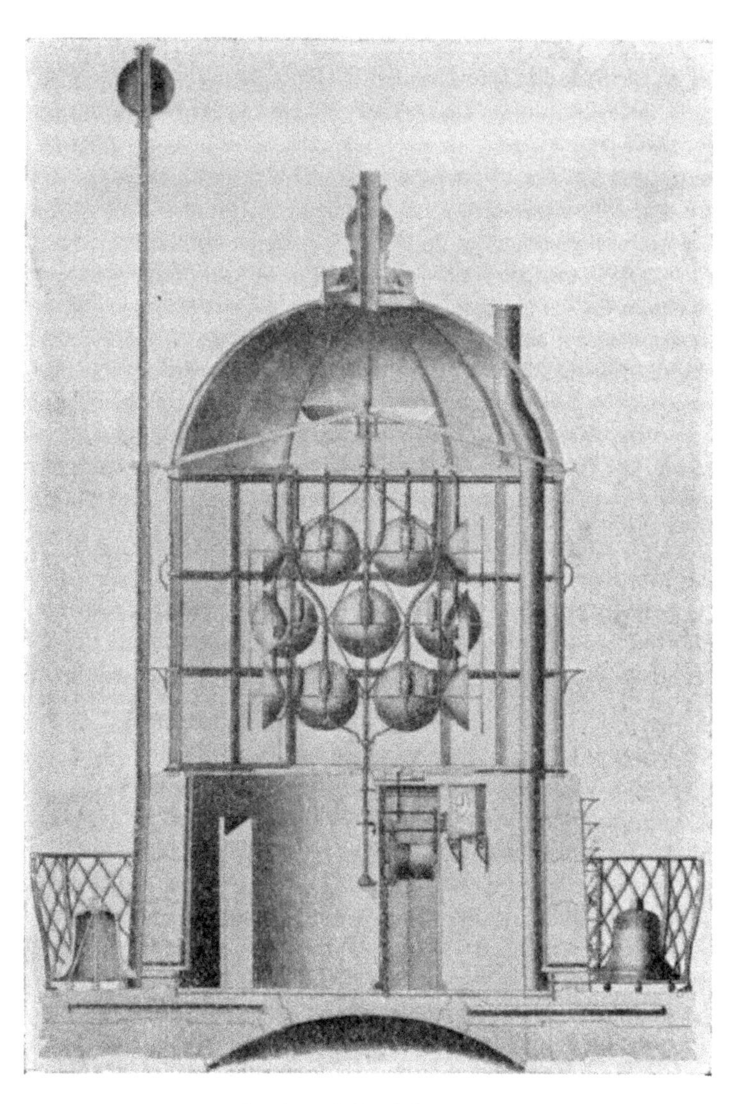

Section of the light-room

of the Smeaton and floating-light landed on the morning of the 25th, when the plumbers and glaziers left the rock: from whom the writer learned the progress which had been made with the work. Among other preparations for the glazing, it was stated that besides the sheeting provided as a screen, all hands had engaged to give part of their bedding for the better defence of the glass, in case it should come to blow so hard as to endanger the stopping of the work. But although the weather had rather a threatening aspect at the commencement of this critical operation, yet it was got through in a manner much beyond expectation, and in one day and a half the light-room was completely closed; though not without being under the necessity of lighting torches at night, which were, however, screened from the view of shipping.

27TH OCTOBER. After the house was glazed, and in a manner externally finished, the writer sailed from Leith for the rock, but as it came to blow very fresh a landing could not be effected, and the yacht was put into Arbroath till the 29th, when the wind became more moderate, and she again stood off.

30TH OCTOBER. On reaching the rock it was found that a very heavy sea still ran upon it; but the writer having been disappointed on the two former occasions, and as the erection of the house might now be considered complete, there being nothing wanted externally excepting some of the storm-shutters for the defence of the windows, he was the more anxious at this time to inspect it. Two well manned boats were therefore ordered to be in attendance; and after some difficulty they got safely into the western creek, though not without encountering plentiful sprays. It would have been impossible to have attempted a landing today in any other circumstances than with boats perfectly adapted to the purpose, and with seamen who knew every ledge of the rock, and even the length of the sea-weeds at each particular spot, so as to dip their oars into the water accordingly, and thereby prevent them from getting entangled. But what was of no less consequence to the safety of the party, Captain Wilson, who always steered the leading boat, had a perfect knowledge of the set of the different waves, while the crew never shifted their eyes from observing his motions, and the strictest silence was preserved by every individual except himself. Under such regulations, which were observed on all occasions of difficulty, the landings at the rock proceeded with the greatest regularity, and by this means safety, and even comfort, were enjoyed where in different circumstances there would have been much peril. The writer is the more particular upon this subject as he conceives that much of the success of the Bell Rock operations depended on the safety which attended the many thousands of landings made in all sorts of weather.

31ST OCTOBER. Having gone over the whole of the low-water works on the rock, the beacon and lighthouse, and being satisfied that only the most untoward accident in the landing of the machinery could prevent the exhibition of the light in the course of the winter; Mr John Reid, formerly of the floating-light, was now put in charge of the lighthouse as principal keeper, while Mr James Dove and the smiths, having finished the frame of the light-room, left the rock for the present. With these arrangements the writer bade adieu to the works for the season.

On one occasion, while the inmates of the lighthouse were standing on the balcony, looking with attention at the wonderful state of the sea, the sprays conducted by the walls came full in their faces, and passing partly over their heads struck upon the second tier of the glass-panes of the light-room, which is

104 feet from the rock! During this gale a thrilling motion was sensibly felt throughout the building, upon leaning against the walls at particular periods when the seas struck the base of the house. The rise of the spray to the height above mentioned rather surprised the writer, as he had not himself at any time seen it higher than about 70 feet. He had, however, felt the tremulous effect alluded to.

5TH NOVEMBER. On Monday the 5th, the yacht again visited the rock; when Mr Slight and the artificers returned with her to the work-yard, where a number of things were still to prepare connected with the temporary fitting up of the accommodation for the light-keepers. Mr John Reid and Peter Fortune were now the only inmates of the house. This was the smallest number of persons hitherto left in the lighthouse. As four light-keepers were to be the complement, it was intended that three should always be at the rock. Its present inmates, however, could hardly have been better selected for such a situation; Mr Reid being a person possessed of the strictest notions of duty and habits of regularity, from long service on board of a man-of-war, while Mr Fortune had one of the most happy and contented dispositions imaginable.

8TH DECEMBER. The Smeaton sailed from Arbroath at 10 p.m., for Leith, to take on board the whole of the remaining appurtenances necessary for the exhibition of the light. She got into Leith harbour on the 9th about midday, when the apparatus was immediately put on board; but the weather was unfavourable for going down the Frith of Forth. Today, however, the wind being west, with a better appearance, the following persons sailed for the rock, viz.; Mr James Dove, smith, who was to screw together the frame for the reflecting-apparatus; Mr James Clark, clock-maker, who had constructed, and was now to regulate, the revolving machinery for the

The exterior of the finished lighthouse, December 1810

lights; and Mr John Forrest, who had the general superintendence of the keepers' duty of the Northern Lighthouses, and, being also foreman for light-room repairs in the service, was to adjust the reflectors and lamps, and remain at the Bell Rock until every thing was found to proceed in a satisfactory manner.

14TH DECEMBER. At daylight this morning, however, the Smeaton was still eight or nine miles from the lighthouse, with hardly any wind. In the prospect of effecting a landing, Captain Taylor manned the boat when about two miles distant from the rock, intending to leave the above persons, and afterwards to take the earliest opportunity of landing the apparatus, the tide being now too far spent for attempting the latter operation. The party thus proceeded, but, on reaching the rock, they had the mortification to find it nearly under water, with such a breach of sea that no boat could approach it. They were therefore obliged to return to the ship, perishing with cold and chagrined with disappointment.

15TH DECEMBER. Most fortunately for the business of the day, the weather was moderate. The passengers went off first, carrying in their boat two cases of coloured glass and a few other articles, while the floating-light's boat followed with the machinery; and by noon the whole of the reflecting apparatus was got safely into the lighthouse.

(On 17th December, 1810, it was advertised in a large number of newspapers in the United Kingdom that a light would be first exhibited on the Bell Rock on 1st February, 1811.)

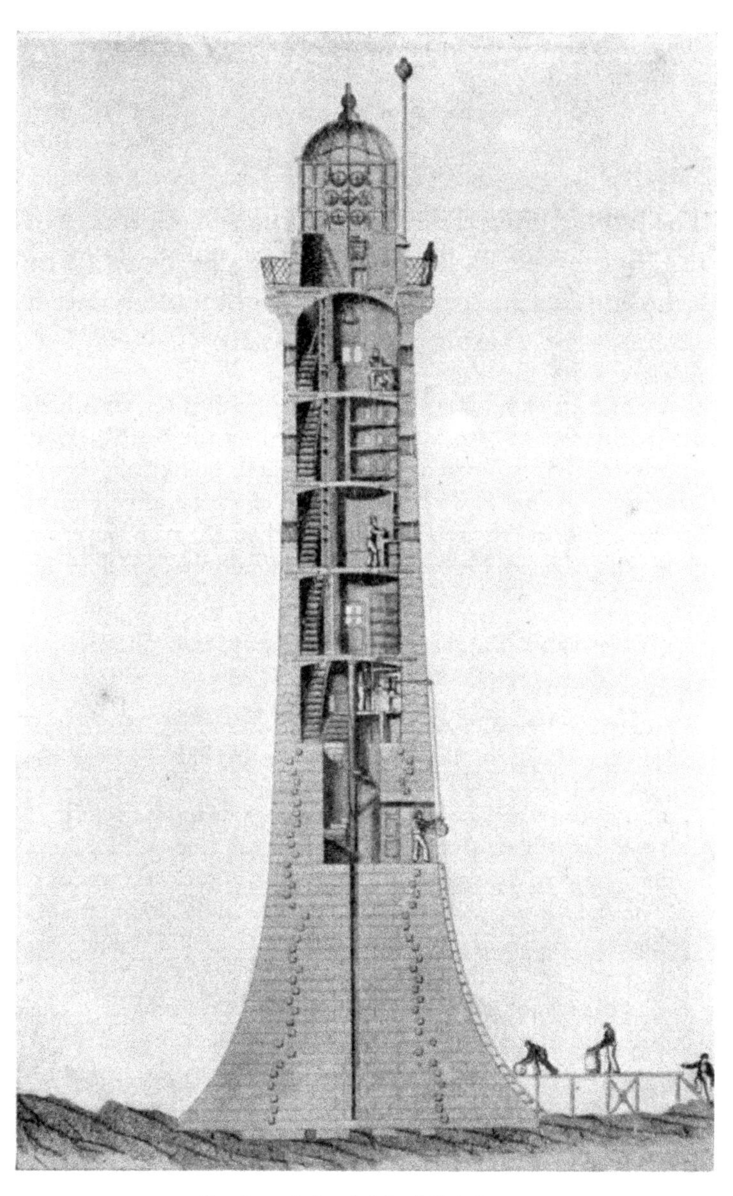

Section of the finished lighthouse

## EVENTS OF 1811 TO 1823

### *CHAPTER XXVI*

# The light exhibited for the first time. Appearance of the lighthouse in a gale. The daily signal. The lightning conductor fixed. The lighthouse painted. Use of carrier pigeons.

1ST FEBRUARY, 1811. The day long wished for, on which the mariner was to see a light exhibited on the Bell Rock, at length arrived. Captain Wilson, as usual, hoisted the float's lanterns to the topmast on the evening of the 1st of February; but the moment that the light appeared on the rock the crew, giving three cheers, lowered them, and finally extinguished the lights.

(In September 1812 the beacon was removed from the rock.)

DECEMBER 1812.

The writer being in Forfarshire at this time was desirous of seeing the effects of the sea upon the lighthouse after the beacon had been removed. He accordingly embraced the opportunity of sailing from Arbroath with the tender, in a pretty hard gale from north-east, at 4 o'clock in the morning of the 9th of December, 1812, and at 7 got close to the rock. The lighthouse now appeared in one of its most interesting aspects, standing proudly among the waves, while the sea around it was in the wildest state of agitation. The light-keepers did not seem to be in motion; but the scene was by no means still, as the noise and dashing of the waves were unceasing. The seas rose in the most surprising manner to the height of the kitchen windows, or more than 70 feet above the rock; and after expending their force in a perpendicular direction, successively fell in great quantities round the base of the lighthouse, while considerable portions of the spray were seen adhering as it were to the building, and guttering down its sides in the state of froth as white as snow. Some of the great waves burst and were expended upon the rock before they reached the building; while others struck the base, and, embracing the walls, met on the western side of the house, where they dashed together, and produced a most surprising quantity of foam. Upon this view of the breaking of the seas at the lighthouse, the frontispiece for this work has been delineated.

1813.

In the course of the year 1813 the light-keepers' houses at Arbroath, the signal-tower, and the sea-wall connected with them, were completed; and a garden of upwards of an acre was enclosed and laid out for the use of the families of the light-keepers, and for supplying the lighthouse and tender with vegetables. The top of the signal-tower is formed into a small observatory, furnished with a 5 feet achromatic telescope, a flag-staff, and a copper signal-ball measuring 18 inches in diameter.

By means of this and a corresponding ball at the lighthouse, certain signals are daily kept up between Arbroath and the rock. The chief of these consists in hoisting the ball at the latter place to the top of the flag-staff, where it is kept, *when all is well*, every morning between the hours of 9 and 10. Should the ball at the rock, however, be allowed to remain down, as is the case when any thing is particularly wanted, or in the event of sickness, the tender immediately puts to sea.

1816.

Owing to the sprays of the sea the colour of the upper part of the lighthouse had become much changed, and had ac-

The Bell Rock Lighthouse in 1930, 120 years after its completion

*(From a photograph kindly lent by Mr David Stevenson)*

quired a dark olive hue, while on the western side the granite courses below were of a whitish-grey; so that the building had now a parti-coloured appearance. To remedy this, and especially to prevent the sandstone from absorbing moisture, it was in the summer of 1816 painted in oil colour of a greyish tint. The whole of the interior of the house being of polished masonry, was at the same time painted white; while the walls and roof of the library were decorated with panelled work, in a very tasteful manner.

1823.

The year 1823 set in with perhaps as severe a storm as has occurred on this coast since the lighthouse was erected. The only accident, however, which happened during that period, was the breaking of the ratchet-wheel spring which keeps the reflector-frame in motion while the machinery is winding up. Though only of a trivial nature, and unconnected with the stormy effects of the sea, it nevertheless created considerable alarm among the families of the light-keepers ashore, as the signal-ball was very properly kept down upon this occasion. Their anxiety, however, was relieved in the course of the day by the arrival of a carrier-pigeon with a billet from the principal light-keeper, intimating what had happened. A pair of these curious birds had originally been presented to the establishment by Captain Samuel Brown of the Royal Navy. They have now multiplied considerably; and two or more are generally conveyed to the rock at every trip of the tender, and let off occasionally for amusement. Their flight between the lighthouse and the signal-tower at Arbroath, upwards of 11 miles, has been ascertained to have been at the rate of about one mile per minute.

*FINIS*

# INDEX

For EU product safety concerns, contact us at Calle de José Abascal, 56–1°,
28003 Madrid, Spain or eugpsr@cambridge.org.

www.ingramcontent.com/pod-product-compliance
Ingram Content Group UK Ltd.
Pitfield, Milton Keynes, MK11 3LW, UK
UKHW010731190625
459647UK00030B/287

* 9 7 8 1 1 0 7 6 1 0 9 3 4 *